1 000+ HINTS for the HOME

First edition in 2012 by
Human & Rousseau
An imprint of NB Publishers, 40 Heerengracht, Cape Town 8001

First edition, first impression 2012

Translator: Vanessa Vineall
Proofreader: Mark Ronan
Designer: Anton Sassenberg
Lay-out and typeset: Wim Reinders
Photographer: Berna Coetzee
Editorial assistant: Lindy Samery
Publisher: Ansie Kamffer

Printed and bound in China through Colorcraft Ltd., Hong Kong
ISBN: 978-0-7981-5498-7
E-pub: 978-0-7981-5659-2

1 000+ HINTS for the HOME

Solet Scheeres

H&R

CONTENTS

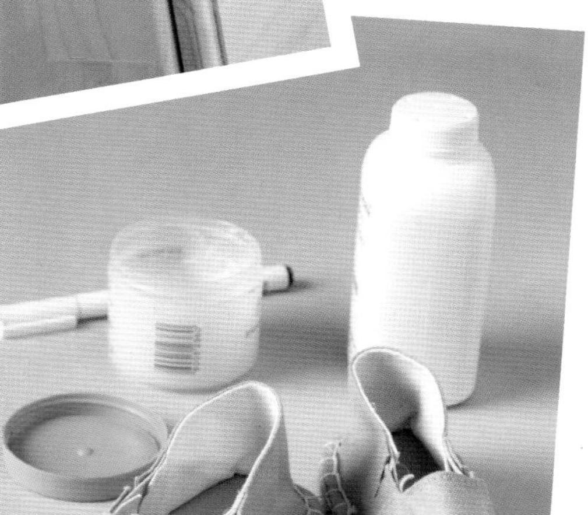

- If you are knitting with different balls of wool, thread each one through a drinking straw before you start. The straws will prevent the different yarns from be coming entangled.
- Place a hot-water bottle in baby's cot when you take her out for feeding at night.
- Make your own medicine kit from a box.
- Write your child's name in each shoe.

Tie a piece of string over the top of the paint tin and wipe excess paint off the paintbrush.

To remove beetroot stains sprinkle borax on the damp stains.

bananas by wrap- them in a damp and storing in a n paper bag.

tarnished silver- e in water in which s have been boiled. with a soft cloth a egar water.

QUARTZ

Get ORGANISED 1

Emmett's Law

"The dread of doing a job uses up more time and energy than doing the job itself."

Rita Emmett

Notice board

Put up a notice board or large calendar in a central place in your home and use it to keep track of everyone's activities, appointments and to-do lists. This will make sure that every member of the family knows what is happening and what to expect.

Three easy steps

Tackling the job of organising your home is a three-step process:

- Evaluate: decide whether you really need that item and how often you use it – be honest!
- Eliminate: donate unwanted items to a charity or welfare organisation, a local bazaar or a garage sale.
- Organise: place things you use often close at hand and those you don't need very often further back in the cupboards or higher up on shelves.

Something in, something out

Make it a habit to get rid of something in your home every time you acquire something new. This will teach you to think twice before making impulse purchases, and stop your possessions from overwhelming you.

Everything in its place

When you have finished with something, put it away. It is far easier to do a little every day than to face a mountain of clearing and sorting every so often.

When you have finished with something, put it away!

Hold a junk hunt

Make clearing up a game. Get everyone in the family to go through the house at the same time, looking for 20 items that can be thrown away. Repeat the game, looking for 20 items to be given away.

Sort out your handbag

Make use of down time when waiting for your children and clear out your handbag.

Shopping list

Write your shopping lists on sticky notes. Then you can stick your list to the handle of the trolley and hit the supermarket aisles at speed.

File important documents and guarantees together in one place.

Advertising breaks

Use the advertising breaks during your favourite television programme to tidy a drawer, shelf or the coffee table.

Paper trail

Place all your household and personal paperwork in one box or container. Then sort it into different types, such as urgent, personal, banking, tax, expenses, schools, warranties and instruction manuals.

Important documents

File important documents and guarantees in one place. Store instruction manuals together in a flip file for easy access.

Baby steps

Every week make just one small change to the way you manage your household. In this way, it will be much easier to learn new habits and shake off those unproductive ones.

Plan

Make time every evening to plan for the next day and avoid morning hysteria. Pack school bags (better still, teach the children to do this), set the table for breakfast and plan what you are going to wear.

Menu plans and doing big shops

Plan a menu for the week before going grocery shopping. This will help prevent impulse buys, ensure you have everything you need when you are ready to cook, prevent unnecessary trips to the supermarket and save time when shopping because you will know exactly what you are looking for.

Delegate household responsibilities to others. A home is not a hotel!

Prioritise

Decide which tasks for the day are the most important, and tackle them first. Leave less important jobs for later in the day and do not allow yourself to become distracted by things that are not urgent or relevant.

Family meetings

Hold regular family meetings to discuss matters such as chores and responsibilities, holidays, emergency situations and security. If children realise that their contributions are being heard, they are more likely to co-operate. This also teaches children the important skill of communication from an early age.

Delegate

If you are not the only member of the household, you need to delegate certain household responsibilities to others. A home is not a hotel!

First make a list

Make a list of everything you need to get done and cross off jobs once you have completed them.

Use an alarm clock

Set an alarm to go off after an hour, for instance, and try to finish within that time. There is nothing like a bit of pressure to help get things done.

Important numbers

Keep a list of important telephone numbers next to the phone or on the fridge. Remember to include the police, your security company, doctor and fire department/emergency services, as well as the number of a relative or family friend the children can call in an emergency.

Use technology wisely

Telephones, cellphones and computers make it possible to work from home. However, technology can also waste an enormous amount of time. Take a close look at how you spend your time in front of the screen and then make an effort to be disciplined and work more efficiently.

No more empty hands!

Never leave a room with empty hands. There is always something to be packed away or moved somewhere else in the house.

Do one thing at a time

It is more efficient to complete one task properly than spend days struggling to wade through a number of jobs at the same time.

Notes

Notes

CLEANING tips 2

Cleaning schedule

Draw up a list of what needs to be cleaned each day and try not to deviate from it. Keeping to a cleaning schedule will ensure that most areas of your home remain clean most of the time.

Water before soap

- Make up a bucket of soapy water for cleaning by first filling the bucket with warm water before adding the detergent. One capful is sufficient: too much soap will leave a greasy residue. Add a capful of ammonia to cut through the grease.
- A teaspoon of washing soda added to the solution also helps dissolve grease. It is kinder to the environment and better for your health.

Power vacuum

Tie a nylon stocking over the end of the vacuum hose. This will attract more dust.

Beat the pong

Spoon a little bicarbonate of soda into the vacuum cleaner bag to prevent nasty odours. You can also use washing powder, but bicarb is more environmentally friendly.

Make them last

Extend the life of new brooms and brushes by soaking them well in salt water and leaving them to dry completely before use.

Skewed bristles

If the bristles of a broom have become bent to one side, you can steam them straight again over a pot of boiling water.

Fix a rickety broom

- Buy a new broom handle. Unscrew the old handle from the broom. Drill a hole the width of the new handle in a square piece of wood. Screw the wood to the broom, aligning the two holes. Then screw the handle in position with a screw through the side of the block of wood.
- Another method is to wrap plumber's tape around the bottom of the broom handle to enable it to be screwed in firmly again.

Soften the blow

Stick pieces of carpeting or foam rubber on the edges of your broom to prevent it damaging furniture.

Stick pieces of carpeting or foam rubber on the edges of your broom to prevent it damaging furniture.

Dripping mop

Screw a strong hook into the end of the mop handle so you can hang it on the washing line to dry.

Disinfect a mop

Soak your mop regularly in a solution of boiling water and white vinegar (spirit vinegar). This will stop bacteria breaking down the fibres.

Make your own dustpan

Use a square five-litre oil can to fashion your own dustpan. Take the section with the handle and cut off the top at a 45-degree angle. Fold over the sharp edges.

Protect your knees

- Wear a pair of kneepads like those used by roller skaters and skateboarders when you have work to do that involves kneeling.
- Make your own kneepads by attaching some 2 cm-wide elastic to a sponge shoulder pad. They are easy to slip on and will protect your knees and clothes.
- Cover a small, flat cushion in thick fabric or plastic and use it to kneel on.

Nail damage

Push cotton wool into the tips of rubber gloves to prevent long nails making holes in the gloves. It will also protect your nails as you work.

Clean chamois leather

Soak dirty chamois leather in buttermilk overnight, then rinse well.

Steel wool

To prevent steel wool rusting, store it in a bottle containing a solution of lemon juice and water with a pinch of bicarbonate of soda.

Stained wash cloths

Boil dirty wash cloths with orange or lemon peel to get them white again.

Banish bad odours

Rinse cloths in a solution of water and vinegar to get rid of nasty smells.

Clean dustbins

Wash dustbins using a solution of hot water and washing soda, then add a little neat vinegar to the rinsing water. Once the bin is dry, sprinkle a small amount of borax into the bottom of the empty bin to help prevent mould. Warning: borax is poisonous so make sure children and pets are not able to reach it.

Practise separating your refuse

Municipalities in urban areas will soon require refuse to be separated. So get into the habit of disposing of organic refuse separately. Wrap organic refuse in two or three sheets of newspaper, dampen the parcel and bury it in the garden – it will attract earthworms which, in turn, will lure more birds to your garden. Organic refuse can also be added to your compost heap. (Read more about compost in Chapter 14.)

Pepper deterrent

To deter cats from digging in the garbage, sprinkle pepper around the dustbins.

New use for old tyres

Place your outside bin inside a tyre to prevent it being knocked over.

Keep that bin closed

Take a strip of tyre and tie the ends to the handles on the lid of the dustbin. This then acts like an oversized elastic band to keep the lid on the bin.

Notes

STAIN-REMOVAL tips 3

The golden rule of stain removal

Attend to stains immediately and do not allow them to set.

General information

- These stain-removal guidelines are applicable mainly to fabric.
- Lightly scrape off as much of the soiling as possible. Be careful not to rub it into the fabric.
- Use a stain remover only if the fabric is stained or if there is a visible grease or oil mark. Otherwise, rinse the item in cold water immediately. Using hot water could set the stain permanently.

Adhesive from stickers

Remove sticker adhesive that has been left behind on clothing by warming the affected area using a hairdryer. Once it is warm, you should be able to roll the adhesive into a ball and remove it.

Antiperspirant

- Use washing soda along with your usual detergent. The washing soda improves the effectiveness of the detergent by creating an alkaline environment.
- Alternatively, soak in a solution of water and vinegar or ammonia. You could also use a little methylated spirits to remove the stain.

Ballpoint pen

- Rub toothpaste on the mark and rinse in cold water.
- Use methylated spirits or glycerine with a few drops of ammonia.
- On suede, carefully remove the mark using fine sandpaper.

Beer

Wash in lukewarm water. Soak stubborn stains in white vinegar.

Beetroot

Sponge with cold water. Soak overnight in water and detergent, then rinse. Sprinkle borax on the damp stain and pour boiling water over it. Warning: borax is poisonous.

Blood

- Dab with a tissue or kitchen paper and leave to soak in cold water until the stain has lifted, then wash in the washing machine.

- Soak stubborn stains in a borax solution made up of one teaspoon of borax in half a bucket of water. Warning: borax is poisonous.
- If the blood has already dried on the fabric, brush off as much as possible first.

Washing soda improves the effectiveness of the detergent by creating an alkaline environment.

Brass and silver tarnish

Sponge off with diluted ammonia or bicarbonate of soda.

Butter

Wash in very hot water.

Candle wax

- Freeze the wax with a packet of ice blocks. Scrape it off, place the item between two sheets of brown paper and melt off the remaining wax with an iron.
- Remove stubborn wax marks with benzene or methylated spirits. Warning: benzene is toxic.

Chewing gum

Freeze the gum with a packet of ice blocks to make it easier to remove. Treat any mark that remains with methylated spirits.

Chocolate

Scrape off the chocolate and wash off in cold water. Soak the stain in a biological detergent.

Coffee

- If you treat a coffee stain immediately it should not leave a mark. Treat old stains with borax or glycerine. Warning: borax is poisonous.
- Stains on washable fabrics can be soaked in a little milk before being washed.

Cola

Rub blue mottled soap on the mark.

Diesel and petrol
Work an absorbent substance, such as cornflour, bicarbonate of soda or salt, into the oil stain using an old toothbrush, and brush off. Then apply lemon juice in the same way.

Egg white
Dab with cold salt water.

Egg yolk
Soak in cold salt water (hot water will set the stain). A stubborn stain can be soaked in hydrogen peroxide and five drops of ammonia.

Flowers
- Wet the stain with water and treat with detergent. Use methylated spirits on a stubborn stain.
- When removing pollen, do not use a damp cloth and avoid rubbing the mark. Brush off the pollen or remove it from the fabric using a piece of sticky tape. Then wash the item in cold water.

Fruit juice
Wash fresh stains in water. Treat older stains with citric acid.

Glue
- Even superglue can be dissolved using acetone. Dab nail-polish remover on the glue to be removed, leave it to stand for a while, then scrape it off with a knife.
- It is important to remember that you can only use acetone on natural fibres. If you want to remove glue from an artificial fibre, harden the glue using a bag of ice blocks or place the item in the freezer for a while. You should then be able to scrape off the glue.

Grass
Treat with methylated spirits, or rub glycerine on the mark and leave to stand for a while. Wash in hot soapy water.

Gravy
Treat gravy stains like blood stains. Soak in cold water and dab with benzene. Warning: benzene is toxic.

Grease
Scrape it off and wash the item in very hot water. Use washing soda and borax to emulsify grease and paraffin to dissolve it. Warning: borax is poisonous.

Hairspray
Soak in hot water to dissolve the spray.

Ice cream
Wipe off the ice cream and wash the item in hot water and detergent.

Ink
- To remove ink from a marking pen, rub the stain with a piece of paper towel dipped in denatured ethyl alcohol (available from pharmacies).
- Remove a mark made by a felt-tipped pen by rubbing glycerine on it, then wash it in methylated spirits.

Jam and caramel
Rinse in cold water, soak in a detergent solution and apply diluted hydrogen peroxide to any remaining mark.

Lipstick
Remove with glycerine, eucalyptus oil or diluted ammonia.

Machine oil
Rub neat detergent into the mark. Treat stubborn stains with benzene. Warning: benzene is toxic.

Mascara
Wipe off with a solution of ammonia and water.

Mayonnaise
Soak in a little water to which detergent has been added.

Eucalyptus oil is an essential oil that can be used success-fully on most oil stains. It is environ-mentally friendly and non-toxic.

Mould and mildew

Remove mould from leather using antiseptic mouthwash.

Mud

Brush off the dried mud and treat with methylated spirits before washing the item in a detergent solution.

Mustard

Rinse in cold water and soak in a detergent solution. Because mustard is often coloured with turmeric, also refer to the tip below for removing turmeric and curry stains.

Nail polish

Place an absorbent layer of paper towel under the item and remove the nail polish using acetone. Stubborn stains can be removed with spirits.

Nicotine

Apply lemon juice to the stain and leave to bleach in the sun. Stubborn stains can be removed with a solution of equal parts of benzene and glycerine. Warning: benzene is toxic.

Oil

- Eucalyptus oil is an essential oil that can be used successfully on most oil stains. It is environmentally friendly and non-toxic.
- Vegetable-oil stains can be treated with methylated spirits to which a few drops of white vinegar have been added.

Paint

- Acrylic: use methylated spirits.
- Emulsion: wash while the paint is still wet; once dry, it cannot be removed.
- Oil paint: fresh marks can be removed using turpentine. For old, dry marks, rub green household soap onto the paint and leave to soak in water for a few hours. Then scrape off the paint using a knife and wash in lukewarm water.

- Children's paint or distemper paint: once the paint has dried, it becomes almost impossible to remove. Treat fresh paint marks with cold, soapy water.

To treat the sweat stains on shirts, drench a cloth in eucalyptus oil and apply to the marks.

Perfume

Treat perfume marks with glycerine.

Rust

- Stretch the fabric over a bowl of boiling water so that the stain is exposed to the steam. Treat the rust mark by applying a solution of one teaspoon of salt in a dessertspoon of lemon juice.
- Rust marks can also be rinsed off with white vinegar. Have woollen and silk fabrics cleaned professionally.
- Sprinkle dishwashing detergent granules over the rust marks and rub in using half a raw potato. Rinse well.

Shoe polish

Treat with benzene or turpentine. Warning: both these substances are poisonous.

Skin oil

Washing soda in combination with a detergent helps cut through oil stains, including those caused by oil from the skin.

Sweat

- Apply white vinegar and dishwasher rinse aid to the stain. Leave it to be absorbed before washing with the rest of the laundry.
- You can also rub green household soap onto the stain and leave overnight before washing normally.
- To treat sweat stains on shirts, drench a cloth in eucalyptus oil and apply to the marks.

Turmeric and curry

- Soak washable items in warm soapy water for half an hour, then leave to bleach in the sun, keeping the affected area damp with the soapy water.
- Sponge down non-washable items with a 50% solution of white vinegar or lemon juice and water.

Vegetables

Treat vegetable stains with a slice of raw potato. For stubborn stains, rub with a neutral-coloured hair shampoo.

Wax crayon

Rinse with methylated spirits.

Wine

- Treat red-wine stains with milk or white wine. Leave to soak overnight and wash the next day.
- Red-wine stains on a carpet should be treated immediately with soda water. If you do not have any to hand, pour a few spoons of salt onto the stain to absorb the wine.
- If the wine stain on an item of clothing is a fresh one, spread the fabric over a pot and pour boiling water onto it from a height of about 75 cm. The wine stain should disappear immediately.

Notes

SAFETY & security

4

Trust your intuition

If a situation feels strange or if you are feeling unsafe or uncomfortable somewhere, leave immediately or obtain help. Your intuition is usually correct.

Be alert

- Change the locks as soon as you move into a new home.
- Trim hedges and trees around the perimeter of your house, leaving fewer places for intruders to hide.
- Do not leave doors and windows open unnecessarily: this is an open invitation to burglars.
- Always lock up the house, even if you are going to be out only for a few minutes. Burglars work fast!
- At night, lock away bicycles, tools and valuable items kept in the garden.
- Do not store ladders in an obvious, visible spot. Do not put expensive electronic equipment where it can be seen from the street.
- Consider having an automatic gate installed.
- Make sure the outside of your house is well lit and install motion-activated lights.
- Install security cameras: even artificial ones will deter would-be burglars.
- Install an alarm that is activated outside the house before being activated inside. This gives you extra response time.
- If possible and if you are able to look after it properly, get a dog.
- Put the emergency number of your security firm and the police services on speed dial on your cellphone and land line.

Safety in the bathroom

- Small children must never be left in the bath unattended.
- Keep the bathroom door shut if you are running a bath and are not able to be in the room the entire time, especially when there are small children around.
- Adjust the temperature of the geyser in order to prevent scalding.
- Install a childproof hot-water tap.
- Bathwater temperature of 35 °C is hot enough for children; 30 °C is adequate for babies.
- Place a rubber bath mat or towel on the bottom of the bath to prevent babies and small children slipping.
- Install a handrail in the bath and in the shower.

Mind the step

Ensure that staircases are well lit. If there are children or elderly people living with you, stick a line of small LED lights along the passage wall to light the way to the toilet and leave it switched on at night. Also make sure that there is a sturdy handrail on staircases.

Prevent poisoning

- Store medicine and poisonous substances on the highest shelf in a cupboard, preferably locked away.
- Lock cleaning materials away in a cupboard or box with a childproof lock.
- Never keep or make up poisonous substances in old cooldrink bottles.
- Do not throw expired medicine or old poisons in the dustbin: rather hand in these substances at your pharmacy.

Smoke detector/alarm

Install a smoke detector in the ceiling of the passage or hallway, ensuring that it is positioned in the middle of the ceiling and not stuck away in a corner. When deciding where to position the smoke detector, make sure you are able to hear the alarm from your bed.

If someone is electrocuted

- Immediately switch off the electricity at the mains. Do not touch the person until the current is off.
- Call an ambulance immediately.
- If the person is stuck to an electrical appliance, try to unplug it.
- Do not touch the person with your bare hands. Put on a pair of dry rubber gloves or use several sheets of newspaper to push the person away from the power point. You could also use a broom, sheet or towel to move the victim.

Put the emergency number of your security firm and the police services on speed dial on your cellphone and land line.

- Put the person on their back and check whether the airway is open. If the victim is not breathing, start cardio-pulmonary resuscitation (CPR). You must never perform CPR unless you have completed an approved course.
- Do not apply any ointments to burns.

Secure your swimming pool

- Erect a high fence around the swimming pool and make sure the gate has a childproof lock.
- Have a net installed to cover the pool.
- Make sure there is adequate lighting around your swimming pool.
- If you have security cameras on your premises, direct one specifically at the pool.
- Never allow children to swim without adult supervision.
- As a swimming-pool owner, it is advisable to do a first-aid course that covers what to do in the event of drowning.
- Always keep a cellphone or portable telephone on hand if people are swimming so that you can call for help in an emergency.
- Keep flotation devices in an obvious and visible place near the swimming pool.
- Teach children to swim early and explain the dangers of water to them from a very young age.
- Remember: do not run near a swimming pool; do not dive in murky or shallow water; and never pretend to be drowning.

Some poisonous plants common in gardens

- A surprising number of ordinary garden trees and plants are poisonous if not handled carefully. Teach children from a young age not to put any plant material – stems, leaves, berries, seeds or roots – in their mouth unless it has been properly identified as safe by an adult.
- Oleander (*Nerium oleander*) is one of the most poisonous plants around. It is also an alien plant in South Africa and can therefore be destroyed without hesitation.
- Most plant poisoning in South Africa results from the use of the seeds of the thorn-apple (*Datura stramonium* or *D. tatula*), commonly known as mad seeds or malpitte. These seeds are a hallucinogen, and teenagers are known

to experiment with them. Malpitte are also found in the muti of traditional healers. Ingesting only a few seeds can lead to poisoning.

Be careful when working with asbestos

Asbestos dust is extremely dangerous and asbestos should therefore not be sawn with a saw. Rather make a groove where you want to break it off using a steel screw. Then press a steel ruler against the groove and bend the asbestos until it snaps.

Test gas cylinders

To ensure that the valve on a gas cylinder is not leaking, place an uninflated balloon over the head of the cylinder. If the balloon begins to inflate slowly, the valve needs replacing.

Remove those lids

Always remove the lids of tin cans completely when opening them. Half-opened cans have razor-sharp edges and can cause nasty cuts.

Fire in the oven

If you discover a fire in your oven, do not open the door. Opening the door will simply give the fire extra oxygen and it will get bigger. Oven doors are sealed, so the fire should burn itself out.

Notes

Notes

the BEDROOM 5

A place for everything, and everything in its place

A clean and tidy bedroom will help ensure a good night's sleep; a grubby mess is the stuff of nightmares.

Good ventilation
To help keep bugs away and prevent mildew, do not store anything under your bed.

Ideal temperature
For restful sleep, the optimum room temperature is approximately 18 °C.

Mattress matters
Turn your mattress regularly lengthwise and from side to side to help retain its shape and make it last longer.

Smelly mattress
For a fresh-smelling mattress, sprinkle bicarbonate of soda on the mattress and leave it for half an hour. Then vacuum up the bicarb.

Urine stains
Remove urine stains from a mattress using a foam carpet cleaner. For stubborn stains, you could also use upholstery stain remover or white vinegar diluted with water.

Protect your mattress
Use a cotton mattress protector under the bottom sheet to absorb sweat. The mattress protector will also stop the sheets slipping.

DIY fitted sheet
Knot the four corners of a flat sheet to turn it into a fitted sheet. Tuck the knots under the mattress.

Buy the best you can afford
Buy good-quality bedding made from pure cotton or wool. Unlike synthetic fabrics, cotton and wool breathe, absorb moisture and are less flammable.

Protect your pillows
Put a pillow protector (an old pillowcase will do) over your pillow before putting on the pillowcase.

Fuss-free duvet changing

1. Turn the duvet cover inside out. Stick your hands into the cover so that you can grab the top two corners of the cover and the corresponding corners of the duvet at the same time. Turn the cover back the right way, covering the duvet.
2. When you shake the duvet out, hold the corners of the cover along with the duvet. This will prevent the duvet becoming twisted inside the cover.

Standard bed sizes

	South Africa	European/ continental	North America	Australia
Extra-small single bed		97 x 201 cm	28 x 52 inches	91 x 191 cm
Single bed/twin single	92 x 188 cm	89 x 201 cm	39 x 75 inches	91 x 203 cm
Three-quarter bed	107 x 188 cm	99 x 201 cm	54 x 72 inches	104 x 203 cm
Double bed	137 x 188 cm	140 x 201 cm	60 x 74 inches	137 x 191 cm
Queen bed	152 x 188 cm	160 x 200 cm	60 x 80 inches	152 x 203 cm
King bed	183 x 188 cm	180 x 200 cm	72 x 84 inches	183 x 203 cm

Easy moves

If you are struggling to move a bed or other piece of furniture over a carpet, put the lids from aerosol spray cans over the feet. The smooth plastic will slide easily and you will not have to lift and carry heavy furniture.

Freeze out house mites

To prevent house and dust mites breeding in soft toys, blankets and cushions, pop these items into a plastic bag and freeze them for a few hours.

Clean toys

Soft toys can be placed in a pillowcase and washed in the washing machine on a 60 °C cycle. You can also wash Lego and Duplo in this way.

Use a cotton mattress protector under the bottom sheet to absorb sweat. The mattress protector will also stop the sheets slipping.

Mosquitoes

Keep mosquitoes out of your bedroom by placing small fabric bags filled with fresh mint on your pillows during the day.

Get rid of tackiness

Remove the remains of tackiness from sticky tape and stickers by rubbing the mark with cotton wool dipped in paraffin. Leave to stand for a while and then rub off.

Fish moths

- Fish moths (sometimes called silverfish) are wingless insects that breed in dark, damp places and are particularly fond of starch and sugar. They pose no danger to humans but can cause a tremendous amount of damage to clothing, upholstery and books.
- Keep damp areas dry with proper insulation and make sure enough air is able to circulate.
- Inspect wallpaper, books and cupboards regularly for signs of fish moth infestation.
- Sprinkle borax behind cupboards and large appliances to keep fish moths away. Warning: borax is poisonous so make sure children and pets are not able to reach it.
- Lavender, camphor, cloves and rosemary will also deter fish moths from moving in.
- Catch fish moths by hollowing out a potato slightly and placing it next to their breeding spot in an open plastic bag. The fish moths will crawl into the bag during the night to get to the potato.
- You could also sprinkle diatomaceous earth, available from organic pest controllers, around fish moth nests. Warning: the diatomaceous earth sold for swimming-pool filters has been chemically and heat treated and is very dangerous to humans, pets and livestock. It is therefore not suitable for this purpose.

Clothes moths

- Clothes moths lay their eggs in dark, damp places. They do not drink water and get their moisture from the food they eat. This is why clothes moths are so partial to clothing that contains human sweat. They are particularly fond of natural fibres, such as wool.

- Vacuum wardrobes and cupboards regularly.
- Have woollen coats dry-cleaned at least once a year to destroy moth larvae.
- If you suspect a garment is infested with moth larvae, wrap it in a wet towel and place in a low oven. The steam will kill the larvae.
- You could also iron the garment with a steam iron.
- Clothing can also be placed in the freezer to freeze the larvae.

Store cakes of soap in your wardrobe to keep insects away and leave your cupboard smelling lovely and fresh.

Plants to control clothes moths

- Scatter bay leaves among your woollens.
- Place blocks or balls of cedar wood in your wardrobe to deter moths.
- Make up sachets of cedar wood, lavender blossoms, dried rosemary and southernwood (*Artemisia abrotanum*), and tuck them among your clothes.
- You can also fill such sachets with cloves, dried orange peel, nutmeg, mace, cinnamon, caraway seed and powdered orris root.

Soap

Store cakes of soap in your wardrobe to keep insects away and leave your cupboard smelling lovely and fresh.

Epsom salts versus mothballs

Sprinkle Epsom salts among clothes when you pack them away, or place a block of camphor in the back of your wardrobe. This will keep fish moths away without the nasty smell of naphthalene, which is also poisonous.

Crease-free packing

When packing expensive or delicate items of clothing, spread sheets of white tissue paper between the layers of fabric to prevent creases.

Storing blankets

When you pack blankets away for the summer, wash or dry-clean them, roll them up and tie with ribbon or rope. They will be easier to store this way.

Welcome guests

When getting a bedroom ready for guests, remember: a reading lamp next to the bed; an extra blanket; a dustbin; hanging space and hangers in the wardrobe; towels; a box of tissues; and a spare toothbrush.

5.1 SHOES

Shoes need rest

Do not wear the same pair of shoes every day. Shoes will last longer if you give them a day off after each day of wear, allowing any moisture time to evaporate.

Buy in the afternoon

To help ensure a better, more comfortable fit, go shoe shopping in the afternoon when your feet and legs are slightly swollen.

Waterproofing

Before stepping out in your new leather shoes, waterproof them by applying animal fat such as lanolin to the soles. Keep applying until the fat has permeated the soles. You can also use a mixture of lanolin and beeswax.

Soften leather

Soften hard leather by rubbing it with lemon juice or castor oil. You can also use olive oil.

Shoes too tight?

To wear in shoes more quickly, pour a little methylated spirits into the shoes at the heel and leave it to soak in for a while. Put on the shoes and walk around in them while they are still damp.

If shoes crack

Hold shoes that are cracking under hot running water while you bend the shoe. Provided the water does not run into the shoe, it will not damage it. You could also rub castor oil into the soles of shoes to prevent them cracking.

Banish odours

For fresh-smelling shoes, sprinkle bicarbonate of soda or Epsom salts into the shoes and leave them to stand for a couple of days before shaking out the powder.

Mark children's shoes

Write the child's name in each shoe. Then smear petroleum jelly over the writing and sprinkle generously with baby powder, and the name will not rub off.

Colour your shoes

You can colour brown shoes black by first rubbing them with a piece of raw potato and then applying black shoe polish.

Darker brown

Make leather darker by regularly applying a mixture of milk and ammonia. You can then apply a little dubbin to make the leather shine.

Boot storage

Before packing boots away, insert an empty plastic cooldrink bottle into each one to prevent folds and cracks in the leather.

Marks on heels

Remove black marks from the heels of light-coloured shoes using nail-polish remover.

Grease marks on shoe leather

Rub the mark with benzene, followed by egg white. Warning: benzene is toxic.

Grease marks on suede

Rub the mark with a cloth dipped in glycerine.

Tar marks on shoes

Remove with benzene. Warning: benzene is toxic.

Protect light-coloured heels

Varnish the heels of light-coloured shoes to keep them looking good for longer.

Smooth soles

Use sandpaper to roughen up soles that are too smooth.

Laces and small children

If your child still struggles to tie his laces, thread ordinary elastic through the eyelets instead and sew the ends together securely. After a couple of applications of shoe polish the elastic will look just like proper laces.

Frayed laces

Stick a piece of sticking plaster around the frayed end of the lace and then dip it in glue or varnish. Leave to dry completely before using.

Make your own shoe polish – heat 150 g petroleum jelly in a dish over boiling water and add 50 g liquid paraffin. Mix well and decant into a glass jar.

Hard polish

Soften hardened shoe polish by heating it gently and adding a few drops of vinegar. As polish is highly flammable, be very careful during the heating process and keep an eye on it at all times. Olive oil also works well, and you do not have to heat it.

Make your own shoe polish

Heat 150 g petroleum jelly in a dish over boiling water and add 50 g liquid paraffin. Mix well and decant into a glass jar. Seal the jar and leave to cool.

5.2 JEWELLERY

Valuable jewellery

Store your precious jewellery separately from other jewellery to prevent it becoming damaged. For advice on cleaning valuable items, consult a reputable jeweller.

Keep it out of the bathroom

Never leave jewellery in the bathroom: steam and moisture could damage it.

How to wash jewellery

- Clean gold necklaces and bracelets in a solution of water and vinegar.
- If the stones are set with glue, do not wash the item of jewellery.
- Bright stones, such as diamonds, sapphires and rubies, are hard and do not absorb moisture, and can therefore be washed. Toothpaste foam or shaving cream on a soft brush works well.
- Coloured stones such as opals, amber, coral and malachite will absorb moisture and should therefore be washed very quickly to avoid damage. Avoid chemical detergents. Clean with water at room temperature and just a drop of liquid soap. Brush off stubborn or compacted dirt using a very soft brush.

Pearls

- Always wipe your pearls with a clean cloth when you take them off.
- Be careful not to spray perfume or hairspray on pearls.
- Moisturise pearls from time to time by soaking them in a saltwater solution for a couple of hours. Note that the silk on which some pearls are strung is coloured and the colour may run if you soak the pearls for a long time.
- Store pearls in a suede pouch and not in wool or batting. The latter causes a build-up of heat, which can result in pearls drying out and cracking.
- Do not clean pearls with any substance containing ammonia.

Handy storage for earrings

Empty egg boxes are the perfect size for storing earrings.

On a wire

- Screw two hooks inside your wardrobe door and tie curtain stretch wire or a cord between them. This is the perfect place to hang necklaces.
- Alternatively, decorate a wooden hanger and screw hooks along the bottom on which to hang beads and bracelets.

Dip the end of the thread for stringing in clear nail polish before you start re-threading the beads from a broken neck-lace.

New use for an old belt

Punch lots of holes in an old leather belt. Use the holes to store earrings for pierced ears and hang the belt in your wardrobe from the buckle.

See-through photo holders

Look out for plastic sheets of see-through pockets for displaying photographs. These are perfect for storing jewellery in your wardrobe as well as other items around the home. Resealable plastic bags are also very useful.

Camphor for shine

Put a piece of camphor in your jewellery box to prevent imitation jewellery from tarnishing.

Broken necklace

Dip the end of the thread for stringing in clear nail polish before you start rethreading the beads from a broken necklace.

Vacuum it up

Struggling to find a small piece of jewellery or contact lens that has been dropped on the floor? Tie a stocking over the mouth of the vacuum cleaner hose and vacuum the area. The lost item should get sucked up onto the stocking.

Buying gemstones

- There are imitations on the market of every gemstone on earth, so make sure you buy from a reputable dealer. Remember, if the price seems too good to be true, it probably is!
- Make sure you are given a certificate to authenticate the source of the stone.
- Ask the jeweller about the origin of the stone. It will soon become apparent if he or she is trying to sell you a fake.
- If the stone looks suspiciously like glass, without any natural cracks or flaws, you should perhaps consult another jeweller before buying.

Cleaning precious stones

Clean gemstones with denatured ethyl alcohol or eau de cologne.

Ivory

Polish ivory with glycerine or wash it in milk. Non-abrasive toothpaste is also suitable.

5.3 CLOTHING

Dust protectors

- Turn old sheets into covers to protect clothes from dust. Cloth covers breathe well and will prevent clothes getting musty.
- You can also protect clothes against dust by covering them with black refuse bags, although you will need to guard against clothes becoming musty because plastic does not breathe. Cut a small hole in the middle of the bottom of the bag to insert the hook of the hanger.

Gloves

Protect leather gloves by rubbing them with castor oil from time to time.

The perfect hanger

A properly covered hanger will last for years and is kinder to your clothes than an ordinary wooden or wire one. Covered hangers keep the shoulders of clothing in better shape and you will not have the hassle of roughness or splinters spoiling your clothes.

How to cover a hanger

1. Fold a strip of foam rubber or cotton batting in half and trace the outline of the hanger onto it, adding a centimetre or so all round. Cut out, cover the hanger and stitch in place. Make sure that you work the stitches securely.
2. Then trace the padded hanger onto a sheet of newspaper, adding 3 cm right round. Cut the pattern in half where the hook is. Now you have a pattern that you can use on different fabrics.
3. Cut out the two halves of the pattern on a double layer of fabric. Sew each pair of halves together on the wrong side of the fabric. Turn through to the right side and slip onto the hanger, with the open ends meeting in the middle. Fold in the edges and close the opening with neat hand stitches.

   You could also contact your local old-age home. Many such organisations sell items made by residents, including covered hangers. Support the aged!

Wooden hangers

- To protect wooden hangers, cover them in tinfoil before hanging up wet clothes. Alternatively, use plastic hangers for wet clothing.
- Wrap old stockings around wooden hangers to protect your clothes from splinters.

Slip sliding away

- Sew or glue a piece of foam rubber at each end of the hanger to prevent clothes sliding off the ends.
- Sawing a groove into each end of wooden hangers will also do the job.

Cover that hook

Prevent damage to clothing caused by hangers with metal or wire hooks by threading a plastic drinking straw onto the hook and trimming the end to fit.

Static electricity

Get rid of static electricity by pulling the garment through a wire hanger a few times.

Protect leather gloves by rubbing them with castor oil from time to time.

5.4 NEEDLEWORK

Threading made easy

Place a piece of white paper under the foot of your sewing machine before attempting to thread the needle. This will make it easier for you to see the eye of the needle.

Cut across fabric in a straight line

1. Lay out the fabric right side up. At the point where you want to cut the fabric, pick up a thread at the selvedge using a pin or an unpicker.
2. Carefully pull out the thread towards the other side of the fabric, forming a thin line through it. If the line is not clear enough, pull another thread.
3. Now you can cut along the tiny holes in the fabric in a perfectly straight line.

Pincushion

- Make a pincushion using scrap material and stuff it with steel wool. The steel wool will keep your pins and needles sharp. You could also use rice or wood shavings for stuffing.
- Place a magnet inside the pincushion before sewing it up to make it easier to pick up dropped pins.

Hot scissors

Dip the blades of your scissors into boiling water before cutting voile and other thin fabrics. The heat will help you cut straight.

Save those trousers

Turn trousers that have worn through at the knees into gardening gear by cutting off the legs just above where the holes are.

All dressed up

Give clothing a new lease of life by changing the buttons or adding some lace or other trim.

Ironing board

Re-cover a worn-out ironing board using the leg of an old pair of pyjama bottoms.

Shoulder pads

If you have an item of clothing with shoulder pads, sew matching press studs onto the shoulder seam of the garment and onto the shoulder pads. This makes it easy to insert and remove the pads, and you can use one set for a number of items. Removable shoulder pads also make things easier when washing your clothes.

Avoid loose buttons

- Make sure that the buttons on a new item of clothing are securely attached before wearing it. Spending a few minutes with a needle and thread is far better than wasting time searching for matching buttons later.
- Dab a little clear nail polish on the threads at the back of the button to make it even more secure.

Floss those buttons

Sew buttons on school uniforms with dental floss, which is much stronger than thread.

Bobbin holder

Store bobbins on a knitting needle and push the end of the needle into a cork to stop them slipping off.

Zip it up

If you are struggling to put in a zip straight, stick the zip to the fabric with two strips of sticky tape and stitch over the tape. Remove the tape once the zip is in place.

Slippery fabric

Place a piece of clean white paper under slippery fabric that keeps sliding out from under the sewing-machine foot.

Multipurpose make-up brush

Use a make-up brush to clean your sewing machine. It is much more effective than the small brushes that come with the machine.

Tape measure

Store a tape measure by rolling it around the spool of an empty sticking-plaster holder, then put the cover back on.

No pins on leather

When working with leather, do not use pins, as the holes the pins make will be permanent. Instead, stick the various pieces together using tape before you sew.

Soap marker

Use small pieces of soap to indicate pattern markings on fabric. They will wash out and leave no marks.

Old blanket

Spread an old blanket over the table before laying out fabric for cutting out. This will stop the fabric slipping and will also protect your table.

Thick fabric

When working with thick fabric that is difficult to sew, rub a candle over the stitching line a few times and the needle will slip through more easily.

Sticking zips

If you have a zip that is sticking, rub the lead of a pencil or a candle over the teeth a few times.

Snipping off buttons

When cutting a button off a garment, stick the prongs of a fork through the stitching in order to lift the button slightly. You will then be able to cut without damaging the fabric.

Button storage

Use plastic money bags to sort and store different kinds of buttons.

Patterns

Use covering plastic when tracing patterns that you intend to use often. The plastic will last much longer than paper.

Sew buttons on school uniforms with dental floss, which is much stronger than thread.

If you want to put in a hem without any stitching showing, use double-sided iron-on interfacing.

Transfer patterns

Make an old transfer pattern as good as new by treating it with laundry blueing. Mix a piece of blueing with 5 ml sugar and a little water. Use the mixture on a brush to fill in the pattern. Once dry, the pattern can be transferred again.

Alter children's clothes

Sew on cord, ribbon or lace to disguise the marks left on fabric where children's clothes have been let down.

Iron-on interfacing for torn pockets

Slip a piece of cardboard into the pocket. Cut the interfacing (such as Vilene) slightly bigger than the torn area and iron it on. Remove the cardboard.

Soluble thread

Use heat-soluble thread to tack tricky pleats and hold lapels in place. The thread will dissolve when the garment is pressed.

Blind hem

If you want to put in a hem without any stitching showing, use double-sided iron-on interfacing. This is particularly useful on curtains that may need to be altered at a later stage.

Appliqué with double-sided adhesive interfacing

Use double-sided adhesive interfacing to affix an appliqué motif to the background fabric before edging it. The motif is securely in place and will not move about while you sew it on.

Impulse buys

Do not be tempted to buy dress material without a pattern. Fabric is expensive, and if you buy too little you may not be able to get more later, and buying extra is a waste. First find a pattern you like, then go to the fabric shop armed with the right information.

Buying fabric

When calculating how much fabric you need, you should take into account the requirements of the pattern, the width and elasticity of the fabric as well as any pattern on the material. The width of fabric ranges from 114 cm to 150 cm. Stretchy material must always stretch over the width of the garment and not over the length, and must therefore be cut accurately. Geometric patterns should match at the seams and for this you will need to buy more fabric than indicated in the pattern.

5.5 KNITTING TIPS

Loose knitting

- If your knitting tends to be too loose, consider using a smaller knitting needle than indicated in the pattern.
- Knit a test piece to make sure that the size of the completed item will still be correct.

Through the eye of a needle

If the eye of the needle is too small for the wool you are using, make a loop of ordinary cotton and thread it through the needle. Then thread the wool through the cotton loop and pull the loop back through the eye of the needle.

Wool or string holder

Make a hole in the plastic lid of a container such as a powdered-milk tin, then place the wool or string in the container. Pull the end of the wool or string through the hole and put the lid back on. Your wool will now be easier to manage without becoming tangled or unrolling too far.

Pipe cleaner

Use a pipe cleaner instead of a pin or spare needle to hold extra stitches. The stitches will not slide off and a pipe cleaner can be used at any angle.

If your knitting tends to be too loose, consider using a smaller knitting needle than indicated in the pattern.

Drinking straws

If you are knitting with several different balls of wool, thread each one through a drinking straw before you start. The straws will prevent the different yarns from becoming entangled.

Neat neckline

Work a double crochet stitch into each knitted stitch when working the neckline of a jersey. Pick up the stitches using a knitting needle.

Reuse wool

Undoing a piece of knitting will leave you with crinkly wool. Get rid of the kinks by winding the wool around a pot and pouring boiling water into the pot. The steam and heat will help straighten out the kinks.

Knitting needles

Apply a little clear nail varnish to the ends of plastic knitting needles that have become rough or are hooking the wool.

Crochet crisis

Thread thin crochet cotton through a bead before you start working to prevent the cotton becoming tangled.

Sore fingers

If you are working on a large crochet project, put sticking plaster on your fingers where the crochet hook rubs them.

5.6 PATCHWORK

Stencil plastic

Buy stencil plastic (or use old X-rays), photocopy the template or pattern you want to use, cut it out and then stick it onto the plastic with sticky tape. Then cut out the template from the plastic using a craft knife. Plastic templates and patterns last longer and are easier to use than cardboard ones.

Needle storage

Use an empty peppermint container with a sliding lid (such as Tic Tacs) to store needles.

Recycling

Recycle old pins and broken needles along with tins and other metal items.

Washed or not?

To help you remember whether a piece of fabric for patchwork has been washed or not, mark washed fabric with a small safety pin.

Dirty iron

If iron-on interfacing or double-sided interfacing has burnt onto your iron, clean it off with denatured ethyl alcohol, available from pharmacies.

Raise your machine

If you struggle to see the pieces of fabric when quilting on a sewing machine, raise the front of your machine slightly using a book or two rubber door stoppers.

Large quilt

When it comes to assembling the different sections of a large patchwork quilt, hang it on the washing line to work on it. It is much easier than crawling around on the floor.

5.7 EMBROIDERY

Align embroidery thread correctly

Embroidery thread is twined in a particular direction. Always thread it through the eye of the needle in the same direction it comes off the skein. If you twist the thread in another direction, you will not be able to achieve a neat appearance.

Keep it short

Never work with a long piece of embroidery thread. The thread will become fleecy and will lose its sheen, and your work will look uneven.

Twisted thread

As you work, regularly lift your embroidery project up in the air to allow the needle and thread to unwind. This will help prevent knots in the thread.

Embroidery frame

- Wrap the inner frame of a new embroidery hoop with a strip of fabric cut on the bias and stitch the ends securely. This will help to hold the embroidery material in place without slipping.
- If you put an embroidery project away for a while, it is advisable to unscrew the frame to prevent permanent frame marks on the material.

Damp cloth

Always keep a damp cloth nearby to wipe your hands before picking up your embroidery.

How to make an embroidery protector

1. To protect the parts of your embroidery material that you are not working on, find some soft, thin fabric and cut it the same size as the embroidery fabric.
2. Cut a hole in the middle of the covering fabric that is smaller than the area to be embroidered. Place the hole over the section to be worked and place the protecting fabric in the frame along with the embroidery fabric.
3. Keep moving the hole as needed so you can work comfortably and the rest of your embroidery will remain perfectly clean.

5.8 LAUNDRY

Washing machine

Leave the door of a washing machine or tumble dryer open when it is not in use. However, do make sure that young children and pets are not able to climb in.

Dirty iron

Clean the bottom of an iron by giving the cold iron a good scrub with toothpaste on an old toothbrush. Rinse with lukewarm water.

Clean a stainless-steel iron

The sole plate of a stainless-steel-plated iron (not porcelain or Teflon) that has become scratched can be sanded to a smooth surface by placing a sheet of fine-grit sandpaper on a level surface and rubbing the base of the iron over it. You can also sand the sole plate with fine steel wool.

Less ironing

To cut down on your ironing, put a tennis ball or two into the tumble dryer. Also use tennis balls when tumble-drying duvets and clothes containing down.

Sorting

Make the process of sorting white and dark washing easier by using two separate laundry baskets. Also look out for baskets with divisions for different types of laundry.

On a chain

Attach a length of chain to one side of your washing line so that you can hang clothes out to dry on hangers. This saves a lot of space and the hangers will not slide along the line in the breeze.

Stretched washing line

When putting up a washing line, attach one end of the line to a short chain. The chain should be just long enough to enable the last link to be hooked onto the washing-line hook. As the line begins to stretch, you can tighten it again by moving the hook along by one link in the chain.

Laundry instructions

Washing instructions	Machine wash in cold water	Use a delicate cycle and cold water	Do not machine wash
	Machine wash in warm water	Use a delicate cycle and warm water	Hand wash only
	Machine wash in very hot water	Use a delicate cycle with very hot water	
Bleaching instructions	May be treated with any bleach	Use only colour-safe, non-chlorine, bleach	Do not bleach
Drying instructions	Tumble-dry low	Do not tumble-dry	Dry flat
Tumble-dry on a moderate temperature	Line dry	May be tumble-dried on high	Drip dry
Ironing instructions	Cool iron	Do not iron	Iron, but do not use steam

If you are worried about fabric softener staining your clothes, add it to the washing machine only once the clothes are completely submerged.

Wind

Put clothes pegs on the bottom of sheets and other large items when hanging them out to dry on a windy day. The pegs will prevent the washing from flapping around in the wind.

Neat pleats

Clip the pleats of a dress or skirt together at the hemline with a clothes peg when hanging it to dry. This will make it easier to iron the pleats later.

Clothes pegs in a bottle

Make a container for your clothes pegs using a two-litre cooldrink bottle. Cut a hole in the body of the bottle as well as a few drainage holes in the bottom. Tie the neck of the bottle to the washing line with twine.

Clothes peg bag

Make a clothes peg bag from a baby's T-shirt.

1. Sew the bottom of the shirt closed. Also sew part of the sleeves closed, leaving just enough space to insert a hanger.
2. Insert a small clothes hanger and pop in the pegs through the neck of the T-shirt.

Grimy shirt collars

- Rub a neutral-coloured or clear shampoo on dirty shirt collars before putting them in the wash.
- Alternatively, rub a paste made with vinegar and bicarbonate of soda on the collar before washing.

Fabric softener stains

If you are worried about fabric softener staining your clothes, add it to the washing machine only once the clothes are completely submerged.

Natural softener

Fabric softener was developed to remove static electricity from synthetic fabrics, but is now often used simply to perfume clothes. It is therefore not really necessary to use softener for all your clothes. Make an environmentally- and skin-friendly fabric softener by mixing one part bicarbonate of soda, one part white vinegar and two parts water. Add herbs to the vinegar if you like.

Fresh-smelling laundry

Give your laundry a lovely fresh smell by adding a few drops of lavender oil to a facecloth and washing the cloth with your washing. You could also try ylang-ylang, orange blossom or eucalyptus oil.

Soap residue

- When doing laundry in hard, brackish water, soap residue may be left on the clothes. Prevent this by adding a quarter of a cup of bicarbonate of soda to the washing water or the soap dispenser of your automatic washing machine.
- If you do not have bicarb, a quarter of a cup of white vinegar in the rinsing water also works well. It is particularly effective for baby's nappies and if your baby has a sensitive skin.

Shredded tissues

If you left a tissue in the washing and everything is covered in white fluff, simply wash the load, adding an old stocking or microfibre cloth. The tissue will stick to it instead of to the clothes.

Soft clothes

Clothes become ultrasoft if you leave them to soak overnight in a mixture of water and white vinegar. Rinse well before washing.

Linen

Wash pure linen on a 40 °C machine wash. Remove from the washing machine at once, hang up and reshape because linen can shrink in the wash. Do not tumble-dry.

Give your laundry a lovely fresh smell by adding a few drops of lavender oil to a face-cloth and washing the cloth with your washing.

Coloured linen

Keep coloured linen bright by rinsing with a mixture of water and white vinegar after washing.

Velvet

Remove fluff from velvet with a velvet brush or a piece of velvet material. Damp chamois leather also works.

Wool

- Pure-wool jerseys should be washed by hand in lukewarm water. Rinse with a small amount of natural softener (see recipe on page 69).
- Press the wool gently to dry. Do not wring, as this will stretch it.

Fluff up angora

The fibres of an angora garment that have gone flat can be made to fluff up again by putting it in the fridge for a while.

A cheaper wash

Use ordinary shampoo to wash woollens. It is cheaper and as effective as expensive detergents.

Stretched buttonholes

Tack the buttonholes of heavy woollens closed with a few stitches before washing to prevent the buttonholes becoming stretched.

Ironing woollens

Use a steam iron on a low setting to press woollens. This will also help make the item lovely and soft.

Hanging woollens to dry

Thread an old stocking through the sleeves of a woollen jersey and peg the stocking to the line along with the body of the garment.

White woollens

Keep white woollens sparkling white by adding a few drops of olive oil to the rinsing water.

Prevent pilling

To reduce the amount of pilling, turn woollens inside out before washing.

Thread an old stocking through the sleeves of a woollen jersey and peg the stocking to the line along with the body of the garment.

Silk

Pour a little ammonia into lukewarm water when washing pure silk. Rinse in water mixed with soda water.

Tea for silk

Wash black silk in tea to help it keep its sheen.

Blue denim

Wash denim in cold salt water to keep it blue.

Remove shine

Get rid of shiny patches on men's trousers by brushing them with vinegar water.

Wet fur

Fur that has got wet can be restored to its former glory by combing it out with a wide-tooth comb.

Sheepskin

Wash sheepskin in a mixture of hot soapy water and 5 ml cooking oil. Repeat until the wool is clean, then hang out to dry.

Feathers

Clean ostrich and other feathers by placing them in a pillowcase with dressmaker's chalk or two cups of fuller's earth. Leave to stand for an hour or so, shaking the pillowcase from time to time. Remove the feathers and shake gently outside before wiping with a soft cloth.

Greying underwear

If you have white underwear that has gone a bit grey, make it white again by soaking it in water in which one denture-cleaning tablet (such as Steradent) has been dissolved. Then wash at 30 °C.

White washing

Use old-fashioned laundry blueing to make whites sparkling white again. Dissolve the blueing completely in water before adding to the laundry or place in the fabric softener dispenser of your automatic washing machine.

Lycra

Do not wash Lycra at a temperature higher than 40 °C. Also add a little fabric softener to the wash to prevent static.

Clean ties

- Place one or two ties in a glass bottle with benzene. Make sure the lid is on tightly before shaking the bottle for a few minutes. Remove the ties, press out the fluid and hang up to dry. Warning: do not inhale the benzene fumes, which are toxic. Benzene is also highly flammable.
- Before ironing the dry tie, cut out a piece of cardboard the same size as the end of the tie. Slip the cardboard into the back of the tie before ironing and the tie will keep its shape without the seams leaving marks.

Easier ironing

Lay a sheet of tinfoil under a loose ironing-board cover with the shiny side up. This will reflect the heat, enabling you to get through the ironing faster. You can also lay it on top of a fastened cover.

Ironing wool

Always iron woollen fabric on the wrong side.

Ironing satin

Iron satin on the right side.

Notes

the BATHROOM 6

It's all relative

"How long a minute is, depends on which side of the bathroom door you're on."

Zall's Second Law

Keep it clean

If you wash out and dry the bath or basin every time you use it, you will not be faced with cleaning heavy soiling or limescale deposits.

Bigger bathroom

- If you want a bathroom to look bigger, choose lighter-coloured or white tiles.
- Choose bigger tiles (from about 30 × 30 cm). Remember, the smaller the gap between the tiles in comparison with the surface of the tile, the larger the room will look.
- To make the ceiling appear higher, choose rectangular tiles and lay them vertically.
- Using clear glass and large mirrors can also add to the sense of space.

Rings around the bath

To dissolve a dirty ring around the bath, dab it with buttermilk and rinse with hot water.

Nasty stains

Stubborn stains in the bath or toilet can be removed using a paste of borax and lemon juice. Apply the mixture to the stain and leave it to work for a few hours before cleaning it off.

Steamy mirrors

- Wipe the mirror with shaving foam, leave to stand for a while and then polish to a shine. Repeat once a month.
- If you do not want to use your shaving foam for housekeeping purposes, you could also use glycerine.

Sparkling taps

Sprinkle a little cake flour onto a damp cloth and use it to polish chrome taps to a brilliant shine.

White towels

Stick to white towels because they can be washed on the hottest setting of the washing machine. White towels can also be boiled if they are very dirty.

Cleaner toothbrushes

- Soak toothbrushes in a denture-sterilising solution every now and then.
- Also try a 3% solution of hydrogen peroxide, an environmentally friendly bleach that gets rid of bacteria on toothbrushes too.

A cup of white vinegar in the toilet will not only whiten and brighten it, but it is also a disinfectant.

Limescale-covered shower head

Soak a shower head that has become clogged with limescale in denture-cleaning solution or white vinegar.

Toothpaste

When you think the toothpaste tube is empty, cut it in half to squeeze out the very last bit.

Remove scratches

Are there scratches and scrapes on your bathroom furniture that is made from plastic or another synthetic material? Polish them away with a little toothpaste or silver polish on a soft cloth.

Ultra-clean toilet bowl

- Pour a tin of cola into the toilet bowl and leave it for an hour before flushing the toilet.
- A cup of white vinegar in the toilet will not only whiten and brighten it, but it is also a disinfectant.
- Pour a packet of tartaric acid into the toilet bowl and leave to stand overnight. Stains should come off without too much elbow grease.

Hairbrushes

Soak hairbrushes (not aluminium ones) in soda water once a month to get them really clean.

Old-fashioned combs

Combs made of tortoiseshell or bone cannot be washed and should be cleaned using a small brush.

Steel wool

Catch hair in the basin or shower before it clogs the drain by placing a piece of steel wool at the top of the outlet pipe. The steel wool can easily be lifted out and cleaned.

Stocking soap

Pop all those leftover pieces of soap into a stocking and tie it to the outside tap so you won't have to walk all the way to the bathroom to wash your hands after working in the garden or garage.

Plug chain

If the chain attaching the plug to the bath or basin breaks, it can be fixed using a key ring.

Slimy sponges

Soak sponges that have become slimy or hard in vinegar or salt water.

Spotless tiles

- When waiting for the water in the shower or bath to get hot, catch the cold water in a bucket and use it to rinse off the tiles afterwards. This will create an unfavourable environment for mould.
- Treat patches of mould with a paste of one part vinegar, one part hot water and two parts bicarbonate of soda. Apply to the mould and leave to dry. Repeat if necessary.

Toilet-cleaning tips

- Place a cake of green laundry soap in the cistern. It is more environmentally friendly than commercial toilet cleaners.
- Dilute tea tree oil and use it to scrub the toilet bowl. Use eucalyptus oil if tea tree is not available.

Win the battle against mildew

Twice a year, wash the bathroom ceiling with a solution of equal parts water and hydrogen peroxide. Hydrogen peroxide is a safe bleach that will not harm the environment.

Good ventilation

The only permanent solution to mildew is good ventilation. Install an extractor fan in bathrooms and toilets without windows.

Keep the curtain straight

Attach fishing-rod sinkers to the bottom of the shower curtain to stop it clinging to your legs when wet. The sinkers will not rust.

Plastic curtain

Shower curtains will remain soft if you wash and then rinse them in water to which a little glycerine has been added.

Nasty smells

- Place a bowl of clean cat litter on top of a bathroom cabinet. You could add a couple of scented candles for decoration.
- Mix your own toilet spray by combining one teaspoon bicarbonate of soda, one teaspoon lemon juice and two cups warm water.

Antiseptic air freshener

Mix 2 ml essential oil (thyme, bergamot, lavender, peppermint, eucalyptus or rosemary) with 5 ml methylated spirits and dissolve in 500 ml distilled water.

Allergy tip

If you suspect you are sensitive to the cleaning materials you use in the bathroom, use cheap shampoo instead. Shampoo contains ingredients that remove grease and other deposits.

Remove limescale

Treat limescale-covered shower doors by scrubbing well with white vinegar. To reduce the problem, get into the habit of drying the shower door with a rubber window scraper every day.

Toilet cleaners

Toilet cleaners are very bad for the environment. Replace commercial products with a mixture of one cup borax and a quarter of a cup white vinegar or lemon juice.

Bath-time pleasures

- Make a small sachet from thin fabric, such as muslin, and fill it with oats, rose petals, lavender and chamomile. Close the sachet and hang it over the tap as you run your bath.
- You could also use fresh rosemary, lemon grass and peppermint.

Recycle soap

1. Grate three cups of leftover bits of soap into a glass bowl. Add a cup of water and one teaspoon glycerine.
2. Melt the mixture in the microwave, stirring regularly. Once the mixture is well combined, stir in a few drops of essential oil.
3. Pour into moulds that you have greased with petroleum jelly and leave to cool completely.
4. Remove from the moulds once the soaps are completely set then leave to dry out on a rack in the sun.

Bath cushion

Use an old hot-water bottle filled to three-quarters as a cushion for your neck in the bath. No one will worry if the cushion gets wet!

Warning: Essential oils

Essential oils are extremely concentrated and can be poisonous in excess. You should therefore use no more than ten drops at a time in your bath. Pregnant women should avoid essential oils.

Make a small bath sachet from thin fabric, such as muslin, and fill it with oats, rose petals, lavender and chamomile.

6.1 HEALTH TIPS

Bruising

Place the inside of a banana peel against the bruise and cover with a cold, wet cloth. The bruising will not discolour as badly.

Plaster casts

- Rub a little petroleum jelly on the edges of a plaster cast to prevent it chafing the skin.
- Sprinkle talcum powder into the cast and blow it around with a hairdryer to help deal with itchiness.
- If the plaster cast becomes very grubby, it can be cleaned with shoe whitener.

Morning sickness

Combine one teaspoon fresh mint juice and one teaspoon lime juice with one tablespoon honey. Take this three times a day.

Home-made disinfectant

Dissolve salt in boiling water and allow to cool slightly. Dip cotton wool in the solution and use on grazes and minor cuts.

Chilblains

Warm chilblained feet gradually and then treat by placing in a warm bath with an extract of pine needles.

Nosebleed

If someone has a nosebleed, get her to sit with her head bowed forward. Ask her to pinch her nose just below the bridge and to breathe through her mouth.

Healthy bladder

Drink a large glass of cranberry juice every day to help keep your bladder healthy and prevent infections.

Reduce the ouch

Rub some baby oil on a plaster before pulling it off and it will not sting so much.

More cotton wool

Make cotton wool go further by dividing it into layers and baking it in the oven at 150 °C. This will puff up the cotton wool and also sterilise it.

Ticks

Do not try to pull a tick off your skin. Rather use a pair of tweezers to grasp the tick as close to your skin as possible and gently remove it. Do not twist the tweezers because the mouthpart of the tick has hooks, and the head will remain attached to your skin. This increases the chance of infection. Keep the tick in a glass jar to show to the doctor if you develop any symptoms of tick-bite fever. Also make a note of the date on which you were bitten.

Bee stings

- Remove a bee sting carefully using the side of a credit card or a pair of tweezers. Do not try to squeeze it out, as this could cause the poison sac to burst and spread the poison.
- Find out if the person who has been stung is allergic to bee stings and whether he has an antidote with him. If so, administer it. If the person is allergic but does not have any medication with him, seek medical attention as quickly as possible.
- Keep antihistamine (tablets and syrup) in your medicine cabinet for emergencies.

Remedies for stings

- Make a paste of meat marinade and apply to bee and bluebottle stings. Handy Andy also works well.
- Toothpaste applied to a bee or bluebottle sting helps to cool the swelling.
- Rub the sap of the sour fig (*Carpobrotus edulis*) on a bluebottle sting. This plant often grows on sand dunes along the coast.
- A paste of bicarbonate of soda and water also helps for bee stings.
- Raw onion helps relieve wasp and scorpion stings.

Thorns and splinters

- Rub a piece of butter firmly over prickly-pear thorns to remove them. Carefully remove any remaining thorns with a razor blade.

- Use ice to anaesthetise a child's hand or foot that has a thorn in it and make it easier to remove the thorn.
- If a splinter has gone in too deep to be removed, draw it out by applying a mixture of Epsom salts and petroleum jelly, and stick a plaster over the top.

Avoid constipation

Improve digestion and avoid constipation by including figs and prunes in your diet. Remember to drink plenty of water.

Basil tea

If you are feeling slightly bloated, basil tea may offer some relief. Pour two cups of boiling water over a mixture of three tablespoons finely chopped basil leaves, one teaspoon grated lemon rind and two teaspoons Ceylon tea leaves. Leave to draw before straining into a cup.

Prevent diarrhoea when travelling

Apply the same common-sense rules you do at home: wash your hands thoroughly before eating and after each visit to the toilet. Also make sure cutlery is absolutely clean and drink only purified or boiled water. Do not drink unpasteurised milk. Preferably avoid ice cubes in drinks and ice cream served from a bowl.

Prevent dehydration

During a bout of diarrhoea, you can prevent dehydration even if you do not have a rehydration product available. Make up a mixture of 0,5 ml table salt, 10 ml sugar, a pinch of bicarbonate of soda and 150 ml boiled and cooled water. Sip regularly until the diarrhoea has stopped.

Improve digestion and avoid constipation by including figs and prunes in your diet.

Reduce puffiness

Add a couple of chopped celery stalks to your salad every day. Celery is a mild diuretic and helps the body eliminate toxins by promoting kidney function.

Sunburn

- Apply natural yoghurt to help relieve sunburn.
- Place cucumber slices or the sap of the cat's tail or snake plant (*Bulbine frutescens*) on painful areas.
- Mix one teaspoon olive oil with egg white and apply to the sunburnt area.
- A lukewarm bath with half a cup of bicarbonate of soda dissolved in it, will also bring some relief.

Minor cuts

Stop the bleeding from small cuts by applying a raw onion. The common garden plant cat's tail (*Bulbine frutescens*) is also very effective.

Minor burns in the kitchen

- Always keep a tube of gel for burns in the kitchen.
- Place the burn under cold running water.
- Cut a raw onion in half and rub on the burn.
- Place an ice block on the burn and keep it there for a couple of minutes.
- Place a cold, wet tea bag on it.
- Treat with a paste of bicarbonate of soda and water.
- If you touch something hot, press your finger against your ear lobe immediately to relieve the pain.
- Apply the sap of cat's tail (*Bulbine frutescens*) to the burn.

Braces and wind instruments

If your child wears braces and plays a wind instrument, ask the orthodontist for extra wax and stick it on all the wires to protect the inside of his mouth while playing.

Basic medicine kit

- Ask your pharmacist to help you put together a basic medicine kit for your home.
- Ensure that it includes:
  - painkillers;
  - disinfectant and a pack of sterile cotton wool;
  - heartburn remedy;

- rehydration sachets;
- diarrhoea medication;
- ointment to treat itches;
- laxatives;
- insect-bite ointment;
- bicarbonate of soda;
- petroleum jelly;
- cold and flu medication;
- antihistamine;
- cough medicine;
- rubbing alcohol;
- medicine measure;
- syringe for dispensing medicine to children;
- antiemetic (nausea medication);
- sunburn remedies;
- thermometer;
- heat pack and an ice pack in the freezer;
- first-aid manual.

Buy a prepacked first-aid kit for your house and your car. Check the contents regularly in case anything has expired and replace it if necessary.

First-aid kit

Buy a prepacked first-aid kit for your house and your car. If it does not come with a list of contents, compile one and stick it on the lid. Check the contents regularly in case anything has expired and replace it if necessary.

6.2 BEAUTY TIPS

Shining hair

Add a dash of vinegar to the second-last rinse to give brown hair extra shine. Use lemon juice for blonde hair. Remember to rinse your hair with pure water afterwards.

Extra colour

Intensify the colour of blonde hair by rinsing it with chamomile tea. Brunettes can give their hair a glossy auburn sheen by mixing henna into a cup of strong coffee and rinsing their hair with it.

Steam for a deep cleanse

Pour boiling water into a bowl and add a few drops of lemon juice and some rose petals. Drape a towel over your head and steam your face for a few minutes. Then cleanse and rinse with ice-cold water.

Cucumber and thyme

Cucumber and thyme have antiseptic properties that prevent infection. Place some cucumber slices and thyme leaves on any red, swollen patches on your face. Cucumber slices placed on the eyes are also wonderfully refreshing.

Mother Nature's scrub

Salt is the ideal ingredient for a body scrub. Combine coarse sea salt with a little bath oil for a scrub that will leave your skin silky smooth.

Avoid sleep creases

If you regularly wake with creases across your face, it is time to invest in a silk or satin pillowcase. Silk will smooth your skin as you sleep on it and help ensure you wake without telltale sleep creases.

Too much foundation

Remove excess foundation from your face with a clean, damp facial sponge. Concentrate particularly on the nose, hairline and around your mouth.

Old toothbrush

Use an old toothbrush to brush your eyebrows after filling them in with a brow pencil. The toothbrush will help smudge any sharp lines.

Flattering eyebrow shape

If you use an eyebrow pencil on your brows, don't draw an arch that droops towards the outside. This will make your lids look like they are drooping. Rather draw the arch with an upward sweep.

Avoid puffiness

Sleep on two pillows if your eyes are puffy on waking. The extra height will help the fluid to drain better from the area around the eyes.

Eggs for a face mask

If the skin on your face is in need of a lift or tends to be oily, whisk an egg white until stiff and apply to your skin. Use the yolk if your skin is dry. You can also add an egg to face masks you make from fruit.

Grape cleanser

Cut a few grapes in half and rub them gently over your face to cleanse your skin. Grape juice is also an antioxidant.

Lipstick on your teeth

After you have applied lipstick, put your index finger in your mouth, purse your lips and slowly pull your finger out of your mouth. The excess lipstick will remain on your finger.

Smooth lips

- Apply a little clear lip balm before your lipstick. The balm will fill in the tiny lines on your lips.
- Dip your finger in lemon juice followed by sugar, then massage your lips with it. This will remove dry skin and leave your lips glowing with health.

Moisturise your lashes

Before going to bed, apply petroleum jelly or baby oil to your eyelashes to keep them in perfect condition and stop them breaking.

Tea-tree oil is well known for its anti-bacterial properties. Apply to your feet to prevent athlete's foot.

Mascara

Extend the life of mascara by screwing the lid on tight and leaving the tube in boiling water for a few minutes.

Furry tongue

If you struggle to remove a white coating on your tongue, up your water intake and chew on pieces of fresh ginger.

Too much make-up

To avoid applying too much make-up, get yourself a mirror with built-in lights. With more light, you can see exactly what you are doing.

Coconut oil

- Use coconut oil to give your hair a nourishing treatment from time to time. Mix the oil with a teaspoon of honey. Apply the mixture to your hair and wrap it in a plastic bag with a towel over it. Leave on for at least 10 minutes before washing thoroughly.
- An olive-oil treatment is also very nourishing.

Spoil your body

Combine rose water and lime juice with glycerine to make a body mask. Slather it on after your bath.

Just like Cleopatra

Pour one cup of powdered milk, one small cup of honey and two teaspoons of jojoba oil into a warm bath. Relax in the water for at least 20 minutes to get the full benefit of this treatment.

Avoid perfume overload

No one likes to be overwhelmed by the perfume of the person next to you, or across the room. Instead of spraying perfume directly onto your skin, spray it into the air then walk through the mist.

Fragrances and their intensities

- Eau fraîche: the fragrance should last approximately two hours.
- Eau de toilette: 20% of the fragrance lasts all day.
- Eau de parfum: 30% of the fragrance lasts all day.
- Parfum: 50% of the fragrance lasts all day.

Multipurpose conditioner

Use hair conditioner for shaving if your shaving foam has run out.

Beat athlete's foot

Tea-tree oil is well known for its antibacterial properties. Apply to your feet to prevent a thlete's foot.

Massage your back

Give yourself a back massage by lying on a couple of tennis balls. Bend your knees and put your feet flat on the floor then move your back over the tennis balls to massage sore, tense muscles.

Parsley for pimples

Crush parsley leaves to a fine pulp and apply to your skin. Leave to dry 10–15 minutes before washing off.

Avoid shimmer

Avoid shiny eye shadow if you would prefer not to draw attention to fine lines around your eyes.

Powder

Use loose powder rather than powder in a compact when applying make-up. Loose powder is easier to apply evenly and it absorbs excess oiliness. Ensure there is adequate light when applying powder and brush off the excess with a large make-up brush. Take a powder compact with you for touch-ups during the day.

Notes

Notes

the KITCHEN

7

The heart of the home

Few places in the home are as convivial as the kitchen. Make yours a place where the family enjoys spending time together. Remember, "Better a dry crust with peace and quiet than a house full of feasting, with strife."

Proverbs 17:1

Blocked drains

- Bicarbonate of soda and vinegar: pour one cup of bicarb down the drain in the sink and then slowly add a cup of vinegar. Follow with boiling water.
- Ammonia and boiling water: pour a little ammonia down the drain in the sink and follow with boiling water. Remember that in the concentration in which it is sold, ammonia is harmful to the environment.
- Washing soda and boiling water: pour two cups of washing soda down the drain in the sink and follow with boiling water.

Powerful cleaner

Make your own cleaning agent that you can use to clean anything from cupboards to floors: combine 4 litres water, 100 ml ammonia, 100 ml white vinegar and 200 g bicarbonate of soda. Keep in a container with a tight-fitting lid.

Effective disinfectant

Make your own disinfectant by combining one teaspoon borax, two tablespoons white spirit vinegar, two tablespoons liquid soap and two cups of hot water. Decant into a spray bottle. To use, spray on, leave to stand for five minutes and rinse or wipe off. Warning: borax is poisonous.

Look after work surfaces

- Artificial surfaces: use an abrasive household surface cleaner to remove stains.
- Granite: wash with a few drops of ammonia in water.
- Laminated wood and other laminated surfaces: use a few drops of eucalyptus oil as a disinfectant. For stubborn stains use an ordinary cleaning product, but do not scrub! Also do not stand hot pots and pans on laminated surfaces for too long.
- Slate: to clean, rub on a few drops of lemon oil and then dry with a cloth.
- Tiles: sprinkle salt on half a lemon and rub on marked tiles.
- Wooden surfaces: make sure you do not burn a mark on the wood with hot pots and pans.

Whiten plastic

If you have white plastic kitchen utensils that have yellowed, whiten them again using this mixture: 125 ml bleach, 60 ml bicarbonate of soda and 1 litre boiling water. Apply, leave to stand for a while and then rinse well.

To reduce the risk of contamination and potential food poisoning, use two separate chopping boards, one for meat and chicken and another for vegetables.

Melamine

Touch up scratches on white melamine with correction fluid.

Chrome

- Use paraffin and a damp cloth to remove greasiness from chrome.
- Remove rust from chrome with bicarbonate of soda on a toothbrush.
- Rub rust marks on chrome furniture with half an onion. Leave the onion juice on the marks for a day or two and then wipe off with turpentine.

Wooden chopping boards

Rub salt into a dirty chopping board using half a lemon. Rinse and then rub the board lightly with olive oil.

Two chopping boards

To reduce the risk of contamination and potential food poisoning, use two separate chopping boards: one for meat and chicken and another for fruit and vegetables.

Keep wood oiled

Rub a little olive oil on wooden boards, salad bowls and salad servers regularly to prevent cracking.

Oven-cleaning tips

- Lay oven foil on the floor of your oven and it will be much easier to clean.
- If food bubbles over in the oven, immediately throw a handful of salt over it. This will reduce smoking and make the mess easier to clean later. Add cinnamon to the salt to mask the smell of burning.

- Clean the oven at once if food has bubbled over. This will save you having to struggle with the mess and grime of baked-on food deposits.
- For stubborn grease build-up in the oven, pour 45 ml ammonia into an ovenproof bowl filled with hot water and heat to 120 °C in the oven. Switch off the oven and leave the bowl to cool in the oven. The ammonia fumes will loosen baked-on grease and grime so it can be wiped off.

Microwave oven

To clean your microwave, place two tablespoons of lemon juice and two cups of water in a bowl and cook on high for approximately three minutes. Remove the bowl and wipe down the inside of the oven using a paper towel.

Polish for oven door

Apply copper polish to the inside of the oven door to remove grease and oil. Rub the glass thoroughly and rinse with hot water.

Use a warm oven

When turning off the oven, take advantage of the residual heat by using it to dry breadcrumbs or bake meringues.

Dirty stove plates

Sprinkle a little white vinegar on ceramic stove plates. Leave it to do its work for a while before washing off.

Cleaning ceramic stoves

Avoid abrasives and, instead, carefully scrape off encrusted, burnt-on marks using a blade. Wash the surface with dishwashing liquid and hot water, then rinse with a solution of water and white vinegar. Polish to a shine with a dry cloth.

Clingfilm

Wrap clingfilm tightly around the knobs of the stove and replace when it becomes greasy.

Lemon cleaner

Rub the cooking surface of a coal-burning stove with half a lemon to remove grease.

Protect the drains

Keep drains clean by placing the shaker part of an empty dried-herb container in the outlet of the sink.

Sparkling dishwasher

Make the inside of your dishwasher shine like new by pouring two cups of white vinegar into the rinse dispenser and running the machine on a short cycle.

Fridge

- Wash the fridge with a solution of bicarbonate of soda and water in a proportion of 1:7.
- Wipe the rubber around the door with white vinegar to prevent mould.
- A fridge that has been standing empty for a long time can be washed out with vinegar. Leave the door slightly ajar to prevent mould.

Sweet-smelling fridge

Wash the inside of the fridge with water to which a few drops of vanilla essence have been added.

Prevent ice

If you have an old fridge that does not defrost automatically, apply glycerine to the sides to stop ice building up.

Greasy tiles

- Use an environmentally friendly alternative to harsh detergents. Dissolve two teaspoons borax, two tablespoons bicarbonate of soda and two tablespoons dishwashing liquid in water. Wash tiles frequently with this solution for the best results. Warning: borax is poisonous.
- You could also use neat white vinegar or a solution of washing soda and water.

How to clean cast-iron pots

- For an environmentally friendly way to clean cast-iron pots, mix a little wood ash with water and use it to scour the pot. This will also protect the pot against rust.
- A less environmentally friendly method is to spray oven cleaner on cast-iron pots and kettles that have become blackened on the braai fire. Apply while the pot is still hot, leave for the time recommended by the manufacturer, then rinse off.

Remove marks from plasticware by rubbing them with a mixture of salt and baking powder.

Stubborn crusts

Clean a stubborn, burnt-on crust in a cast-iron pot by boiling three tablespoons bicarbonate of soda and one cup of water in the pot. Then wash with dishwashing liquid and hot water. Dry thoroughly before rubbing on some cooking oil.

Burnt pans

Clean a very burnt pan by pouring a little olive oil into the pan and heating it slightly. Leave to stand for several hours then pour out the oil and wash the pan.

Rust spots in pots and pans

Sprinkle dishwasher detergent granules on the rusted areas and rub with half a raw potato. Rinse well before washing.

Dishes with burnt-on marks

- Press half a lemon in salt and use to scrub heat-resistant glass dishes.
- You can also clean glass dishes with a cleaning agent for glass stovetops.

Cleaning plastic

- Remove marks from plasticware by rubbing them with a mixture of salt and baking powder.
- You can also remove stains by soaking the plastic cup or bowl in a solution of water and denture cleaner or sterilising liquid for babies' bottles.

Aluminium cookware

- Clean aluminium pots by boiling apple or lemon peel in a few cups of water in the pot.
- Restore the shine to pots and pans with this mixture: combine eight tablespoons cream of tartar, eight tablespoons bicarbonate of soda, 125 ml white vinegar and four tablespoons soap flakes. Apply with a sponge and rinse well afterwards.

Nonstick pans

Once the surface of a nonstick pan has been damaged and starts to peel off, do not use it again. Pieces of the coating can come off during cooking and end up in your food. Most nonstick pans have a Teflon coating, which can start to warp at as low a temperature as 150 °C. Rather choose one that is coated with Thermolon, which can withstand temperatures of up to 450 °C.

- Do not heat an empty Teflon-coated pan. An empty pan gets too hot very quickly.
- Do not scour nonstick pans with an abrasive detergent or sponge.
- Read the pan's care instructions carefully and follow them.

Shiny cutlery

Soak stainless-steel cutlery in neat vinegar for half an hour. Rinse, then polish to a shine. It is a good idea to test a small, inconspicuous spot on the cutlery first to check that the vinegar does not discolour it.

Silver cutlery

- Leave silverware to soak in water in which eggs have been boiled and the tarnish will soon disappear. Afterwards, rub with a soft cloth and vinegar water.
- Keeping a piece of camphor in the drawer where silver cutlery is stored will also prevent it tarnishing.

Once the surface of a nonstick pan has been damaged and starts to peel off, do not use it again.

Silver teapots

Remove tannin stains from a silver teapot by putting six squares of tinfoil in the pot. Spoon in one teaspoon bicarbonate of soda and pour boiling water over the top. Leave to cool and rinse out.

Stained teapots

- Get rid of tea stains in a china teapot by leaving a tablespoon of bicarbonate of soda in boiling water to stand in the pot for a few minutes.
- Use denture cleaner for pots that have been heavily stained by coffee.
- Alternatively, mix one part borax with eight parts water and leave to stand in the pot. Rinse thoroughly – borax is poisonous.

Limescale in a kettle

- Remove limescale and brown stains from a plastic kettle by boiling lemon juice and water in it.
- Vinegar in water is a good alternative to lemon juice. Make sure you rinse the kettle well and boil clean water in it a couple of times afterwards.

Stained cups

Remove stains from teacups and mugs with lemon juice.

Stainless steel

Clean marks off stainless steel using a little methylated spirits on a dry cloth. Rinse well before use.

Tacky Tupperware

Apply a paste of bicarbonate of soda to older Tupperware containers that have become tacky. Leave to stand overnight and wash well.

Musty pottery

Earthenware or pottery that is not used regularly can start to smell musty. Rinse with hot, diluted vinegar.

Beer glasses

If you enjoy a smooth, even head on your beer, do not wash the glasses in soap. Rather use hot water with a little lemon juice in it.

Bread tin
Wash out the bread tin once a week with water to which a little vinegar has been added.

Crystal clear
Immerse crystal in a solution of one part vinegar to two parts water. Dry with a cloth that does not shed fluff.

Antique china
Lay a tea towel in the bottom of the sink before putting antique china in the water to wash. This will help prevent it getting damaged.

Gold-leafed china
Avoid using washing soda or soap powder on porcelain with gold-leaf detail. Rather put a few drops of borax into the rinsing water. China with gold leaf should not be washed in a dishwasher.

Coffee maker
Clean a coffee maker by running a solution of water and vinegar through it. Rinse with clean water before using it again.

Rusted knife
Leave a knife with a rusted blade in linseed oil for a few hours. Then sand the blade lightly with sandpaper.

Marks on blades
Rub marks on a knife blade with half a raw potato or salt and lemon juice. Then rub the blade gently with a scouring sponge.

Get rid of tea stains in a china teapot by leaving a tablespoon of bicarbonate of soda in boiling water to stand in the pot for a few minutes.

7.1 MEAT AND FISH

Temperatures and dangers

100 °C	Boiling point of water. At this temperature, most bacteria in food are destroyed through cooking.
60–74 °C	At this temperature, food is warmed up, but some bacteria will survive.
4–60 °C	Keeping food at this temperature for any length of time or warming it only to this temperature is dangerous because it creates the ideal breeding ground for bacteria, including those that cause food poisoning.
0 °C	Freezing point of water.
-12 °C	Below this temperature bacteria will generally stop multiplying.

Meat bought at the supermarket

- Always select your meat last, just before joining the queue at the till.
- Make sure that the meat is not packed in the shopping with hot or warm items.
- If it is a hot day and your car is air-conditioned, keep the meat in the car rather than the boot.
- If the journey home takes more than an hour, take a cooler bag and ice bricks to the supermarket with you for the meat.

Raw meat

Meat in plastic packaging goes off quickly because the liquid that comes out of the meat can cause bacteria to grow on the plastic. Rather store meat in the fridge in a ceramic or other non-porous dish, covered with greaseproof paper or clingfilm.

Keep them separate

Do not work with raw and cooked meat on the same surface at the same time. Wash a dish thoroughly if it has had raw meat in it before using it for cooked food.

Frozen meat

- The best and safest way to defrost meat and ensure optimum quality, is to defrost it in the fridge. If you are pressed for time, use the microwave.

- Once meat has been defrosted, it can be kept safely in the fridge for a maximum of 48 hours. Do not refreeze because more moisture is lost every time it is defrosted. The quality and nutritional value decline. And very time meat is reheated the chances increase of bacteria multiplying in it.

Liver

- Place liver in a dish of boiling water and leave it to cool. This makes the liver less watery and it is easier to pull the membranes off. Even just dipping the liver in boiling water helps the membranes come off more easily.
- Dip liver in milk and then in flour before cooking it. Marinate liver in milk or buttermilk to make it extra tender.

Beef tongue

Cook tongue in a mould in which puddings are steamed. Use the leftover water to make aspic.

Tripe

Add lemon juice to the water in which tripe is cooked in order to reduce the unpleasant smell. The lemon will also help the tripe soften more quickly

Boerewors

Add extra zing to the flavour of supermarket boerewors by injecting a little vinegar into the sausage before cooking using a clean syringe.

Sizzling sausages

Dip sausages in milk before putting them on the braai to prevent the skins bursting. When they are on the braai, do not prick sausages too much or they will dry out.

Hard biltong

If biltong has become too hard, leave it in the bread bin with some fresh bread for a day or two.

Mouldy biltong

- If it rains incessantly you can hang wet biltong in front of an electric fan until a hard crust forms around the meat. This will stop it going mouldy.
- Biltong that is only slightly fusty can be washed off with vinegar water and then hung up again to dry. In coastal areas, biltong, and especially soft biltong, should be kept in the fridge or freezer.

Moulded brawn

Allow brawn to set in a two-litre cooldrink bottle that has had the top cut off. The brawn will then be in the shape of a meat roll.

Marrow bones

Prevent the marrow running out of marrow bones during the cooking process by inserting "corks" cut from carrots on either side.

Skim fat off soup

Make it easier to remove the fat from the top of soup or gravy by running an ice block over the surface. The fat will coagulate and it will be easier to skim off.

Meatballs

Use an ice-cream scoop to shape meatballs that are all the same size.

Plastic "gloves"

Keep your hands clean by sticking them into plastic bags before making meatballs or meatloaf.

Bread with the roast

Put pieces of bread in the roasting pan to absorb some of the fat and reduce smoking when roasting meat in the oven. This also reduces the likelihood of the fat catching alight.

Brown meat

Brown the meat for a stew before adding the liquid. This will give the dish more flavour and better colour.

Freeze for later

Prepare more stew than you need and freeze the rest for later.

Stuffing safety

Stuffing meat or poultry too far in advance can allow bacteria to multiply. Rather make the stuffing ahead of time if necessary, keep it in the fridge and then stuff the meat just before cooking.

Double up on the gravy

- When making gravy for a roast, make double the quantity and freeze the rest to enjoy later with the leftover meat.
- Give gravy a rich brown colour by adding a little sugar when making it.

Crumbed meat

Put flour or crumbs into a plastic bag and add the meat. Tie a knot in the top of the bag and shake well to ensure an even distribution of crumbs on the meat.

Stop oil spattering

- Pat the meat dry with a paper towel before placing it in the pan.
- Allow meat that has been crumbed to stand for 20–30 minutes before putting it in the pan.
- Make sure the utensils you use in the pan are also dry.

Marinate in wine

- A red-wine marinade made with garlic, onion, bay leaves, thyme and red wine is delicious with beef and lamb.
- Marinate pork in a marinade of white wine (or apple juice), onion, garlic, ginger and curry powder.

Flavouring chicken

Place a whole unpeeled onion in the cavity of an uncooked chicken when storing it in the fridge.

Chicken for pie

Stretch chicken meat for a pie by adding noodles and a tin of mushrooms. You can also use fresh mushrooms, sago or any seasonal vegetables.

Plucking tip

It is easier to pluck the feathers from a slaughtered bird if you plunge the carcass into boiling water first.

To test whether fish is fresh, press it with your finger. If it does not spring back, the fish is no longer fresh.

Drunken chicken

1. Place a whole chicken upright on a full, open beer can so that part of the can is inside the bird. Rub the chicken with oil and herbs.
2. Stand the can with the chicken in a saucepan or a grill pan and place on the fire.
3. Move the coals around so that the heat comes from the sides and not directly from below the chicken.
4. The chicken will be done in approximately two hours or once the juices run clear.
5. Discard the can and enjoy the deliciously moist chicken.

Salmon versus salmon trout

- Salmon is a pink-fleshed sea fish that is imported to South Africa from the northern hemisphere at great expense.
- Salmon trout, on the other hand, is a freshwater fish that is bred locally and is therefore considerably cheaper. The two types of fish are similar in taste, and in their smoked form salmon trout is a good substitute for salmon.

Fresh fish

- To test whether fish is fresh, press it with your finger. If it does not spring back, the fish is no longer fresh.
- Ensure that the gills are red and damp. The eyes must also be shiny and not sunken. If the fish smells fishy, it is no longer fresh.

Fish smell on pans

- After using a pan to cook fish, rub it well with half a lemon before washing as usual and the fish smell will be gone. The same applies to the smell of fish on your hands.

- Another way of getting rid of a fish smell on your hands, is to rub your hands over a stainless-steel surface such as an empty sink.

Fresh mussels

- Hold the mussel under a stream of cold water with the rounded part facing upwards. Tap the shell with a sharp knife. If the shell shuts tightly it means the mussel is still alive and can therefore be eaten. If the mussel remains open, throw it away.
- Similarly, mussels that do not open when cooked should not be eaten.

How to store mussels

Wash mussels in cold water before storing in a plastic bag in the fridge for at most one day. Raw mussels cannot be frozen. White mussels that you have harvested yourself should be placed in fresh sea water first to remove the sand. Remember that you need a permit to collect both white and black mussels.

How to prepare fish

- Wash the fish and pat it dry with a paper towel. Place in a clean plastic bag and store on a bed of ice blocks in a flat dish until needed.
- If the fish is frozen, defrost in the fridge overnight. Rinse and dry gently but thoroughly with a paper towel.
- Do not overcook fish, otherwise it will become dry and tasteless.

No refrigeration

If you do not have access to a fridge, fish will last longer if you rub it with salt, wrap it in a cloth and store in a cool place.

Calamari

Calamari becomes tough if it is cooked for too long: a couple of minutes is plenty.

Hold the mussel under cold water with the rounded part facing upwards. Tap the shell with a knife. If the shell shuts tightly the mussel is alive and can therefore be eaten. If the mussel remains open, throw it away.

Salted fish

Salted fish, such as herring or anchovies, can be soaked in milk to get rid of most of the saltiness.

Custard powder for fish

Add a dash of custard powder to the flour in which you dip fish to give it a lovely colour. You could also add a touch of turmeric for colour. Season the flour with salt and pepper or some fish spice.

Vinegar with the oil

Add 10 ml vinegar to the oil in which you fry fish to stop the fish breaking up.

7.2 VEGETABLES

Peels and all

Peel vegetables over a few sheets of newspaper then wrap up the peels in the paper, dampen the package and bury it in the garden. Doing this means you can clean your work surface in an instant and boost the compost in your garden at the same time.

ASPARAGUS

This way up

Always open a tin of asparagus spears from the bottom to avoid damaging the soft tips of the asparagus.

White asparagus

Peel fresh white asparagus easily using a vegetable peeler.

Fresh asparagus

Wrap asparagus in a damp cloth and store it in the vegetable drawer of the fridge.

BEANS

Softer faster

Dried beans will cook faster if you put them in the freezer overnight and then soak them in water for a day. You can also soak them in boiling water, leave to cool and then cook normally.

Retain the colour

Blanch green beans before frying, stir-frying or grilling and they will retain their lovely green colour.

Green beans

To liven up the flavour of green beans, add a dash of lemon juice to the cooking water or steam them in coconut milk.

If carrots are difficult to scrape, boil them for a few minutes and leave to cool.

BEETROOT

Roots and all

Leave part of the stem and the entire root on the beetroot during cooking. Plunge the cooked beetroot into cold water then pull off the skin and remove the stem and root. Store cooked beetroot in the fridge and slice just before serving.

Gorgeous colour

To retain the colour of beetroot, add 5 ml vinegar, half a teaspoon of sugar and a pinch of salt to the cooking water.

Raw beetroot

Grate raw beetroot into salads: it is deliciously sweet and even healthier than cooked beetroot.

BRINJAL

Slice the brinjal, sprinkle with salt and leave for a few minutes. Rinse off the salt as well as the water that forms on the surface. The salt stops the brinjal going black during cooking, draws out water and helps the brinjal absorb less oil during cooking. Slicing brinjal lengthwise also reduces the amount of oil absorbed during cooking.

CABBAGE

Keep it fresh for longer

If you do not have access to a fridge, cabbage can be kept for a few days longer by chopping it up finely and mixing it with 25 g salt for every 500 g cabbage. Store in preserving jars that close tightly. Rinse off the salt before using the cabbage.

Cabbage and bananas

Cooking cabbage with an overripe banana gives the cabbage a delicious flavour.

CARROTS

How to store carrots

Cut off all but about 3 cm of the carrot tops before storing in the fridge to prevent the green tops drawing moisture from the root (the part that is usually eaten). Carrots also stay firmer for longer in an airtight container in the fridge. Store unwashed carrots with the tops intact by covering with clean sand and storing in a dark place. You can also "plant" the carrots in the garden until you need them.

Easy peeling

If carrots are difficult to scrape, boil them for a few minutes and leave to cool. The skin will now come off easily and your hands will not get stained orange.

Carrot chips

Cut carrots down the length (thicker ones can be cut a few times) and then into batons about 5 cm long, like potato chips. Place on a baking tray in a single layer and brush lightly with oil. Bake at 200 °C until crisp.

CAULIFLOWER

Dash of vinegar

A little vinegar added to the cooking water will keep cauliflower white.

Yellow cauliflower

Old cauliflower that has yellowed can be revived by adding some milk to the cooking water.

Odour

If the smell of cooked cauliflower is offensive, place a slice of bread on top of the cauliflower.

Aluminium pot

Cooking cauliflower in an aluminium pot causes a chemical reaction that will make the cauliflower discolour.

CUCUMBERS

Braised cucumber

Peel two cucumbers, quarter and remove the pulp. Melt one tablespoon butter in a pan and braise the cucumber over a medium heat for five minutes. Add a pinch of salt, a teaspoon of lemon juice and a pinch of mint.

GARLIC

Reduce the pong

Avoid some of the lingering odour associated with eating garlic by not using the green part in the centre. If there is no green core, a sprig of parsley or parsley capsules can help reduce the odour.

Heavy-handed with the garlic

If you have put too much garlic into a dish, add a handful of chopped parsley to the cooked dish (do not cook the parsley).

String of garlic

Thread a number of garlic cloves onto string and hang the string in the food you are cooking. Remove before serving. The garlic flavour will be less intense and you can reuse the string a few times.

Garlic for the bowl

Rub a serving dish or salad bowl with a peeled garlic clove before putting the food into the dish or making the salad. This imparts a subtle garlic flavour.

Finely chopped

The finer the garlic is crushed or chopped, the stronger the flavour.

Garlic salt

Crush a garlic clove until very fine and mix with salt. Leave to dry on a chopping board before storing in an airtight jar.

Garlic oil

- Peel a number of bulbs of garlic, pack the cloves into a sterilised glass jar and fill with hot olive oil.
- Garlic bulbs can also be baked until soft and caramelised. Squeeze out the cloves and preserve in olive oil.

LETTUCE

Tear, don't cut

Tear the leaves from a head of lettuce. Leaves that are cut tend to go brown quickly. If you have to cut lettuce, use a stainless-steel knife.

Rotten apple

Store salad greens away from fruit such as apples that give off ethylene and will cause the lettuce to discolour.

Limp lettuce

Revive limp lettuce by putting it in a solution of cold water and half a teaspoon of sugar for a few minutes.

Storage

Store lettuce in the fridge by placing the head on a paper towel in an airtight container. Washed leaves can be stored in a plastic bag, also in the fridge.

Cooking oil

A few drops of cooking oil added to finely chopped lettuce leaves used to garnish platters of snacks should keep the lettuce from wilting.

MEALIES

How to cook mealies

Adding salt to the water when cooking mealies makes them tough: rather add a teaspoon of sugar. Once the water has come to the boil again and the kernels turn glassy, the mealies are done. Cooking mealies for too long diminishes their flavour.

> Do not rinse mushrooms; rather wipe off the dirt or growing medium using a soft cloth.

Mealie snack

For a delicious savoury snack, cook mealie kernels or frozen corn in oil, drain and sprinkle with salt.

Lump-free porridge

To prevent mealie meal going lumpy, mix the dry porridge with cold water in the pot and then place on the heat.

Mixed grains

Stop mealie meal boiling over and make the texture more interesting by combining one part mealie meal with four parts oats.

Soak overnight

Soak mealie meal in water overnight to reduce the cooking time the next morning.

Mealie tea

Steep mealie beards in boiling water to make a tea that is said to soothe bladder and kidney complaints.

MUSHROOMS

Even slices

Use an egg cutter to cut mushrooms into even slices.

Wipe clean

Mushrooms absorb water very easily, which affects the taste. Do not rinse mushrooms; rather wipe off the dirt or growing medium using a soft cloth.

Avoid foil

White mushrooms will blacken and discolour when wrapped in tinfoil.

ONION

How to peel onions

Cut off both ends of the onions and place in boiling water for 10 minutes. Remove one onion at a time, squeeze the sides and the centre will pop out.

Stop onions sprouting

Cut off the roots of the onion and rub the cut end on a hot stove plate or scorch it with a flame. The onion will not sprout.

To get rid of the smell of onions on your hands, rub a stainless-steel spoon between your hands under a running tap like a bar of soap.

Whole onions

When cooking whole onions, make a cross in the fat end before putting it in the water.

Chop onions without tears

- Use a razor-sharp knife and do not press on the onion while cutting.
- Put the onion in the fridge overnight before chopping.
- Peel the onion, rinse it and then cut it in half lengthwise and place on the chopping board. Chop the onion from the top, cutting off the root last.
- Chew chewing gum or breathe through your mouth and not your nose while chopping.
- Hold a match in each corner of your mouth with the head to the outside. The chemicals in the head of the match will absorb the onion fumes.

Get rid of the smell

To get rid of the smell of onions on your hands, rub a stainless-steel spoon between your hands under a running tap like a bar of soap.

PEAS

Frozen goodness

Peas freeze exceptionally well so if fresh peas are not available, you can be assured that frozen ones are just as nutritious.

Snacks

Make a delicious hors d'oeuvre by lightly cooking pea pods and filling them with flavoured cream cheese.

Pea stock

Pea stock is a delicious base for hot or cold soup. Make your own by cooking the pods, liquidising them and then putting the pulp through a sieve to remove the coarse fibres.

Dunking potatoes that have been cooked with the skins on in ice-cold water briefly will make it easier to remove the skins.

POTATOES

Quicker cooking

Make delicious potatoes quickly in the microwave. Prick the potatoes with a fork to prevent them bursting and place on a plate in the microwave. Depending on the size, one potato will cook in two minutes on 100% power. Turn the potatoes halfway through the cooking time so that they cook evenly.

Better taste

Add a spoonful of sugar to the cooking water to improve the taste of old potatoes.

Easy peeling

Dunking potatoes that have been cooked with the skins on in ice-cold water briefly makes it easier to remove the skins.

Wrinkled potatoes

Soak potatoes that have gone a bit wrinkly in cold water for a while before peeling them.

Potato salad

When making potato salad, do not cook the potatoes for too long (they should not start breaking up). Pour the sauce over the potatoes while they are still warm to enable the flavours to penetrate the potatoes.

Crispy potatoes

Make extra-crispy roast potatoes by sprinkling them with flour halfway through the cooking time.

Quick roast potatoes

Par-cook potatoes in the microwave before finishing them off in oil on the stove.

Storing potatoes

- Store potatoes in a dark place to stop them going green.
- You can keep potatoes for up to six months by placing them in a bucket and covering them with clean, dry sand. Put a lid on the bucket and store it in a cool place.

Mashed potatoes

Add a little baking powder and milk to mashed potatoes to make them light and creamy.

PUMPKIN

Keep it fresh

Keep the unused half of a pumpkin fresh by sprinkling the cut side with sugar or caster sugar.

Microwave pumpkin

You can cook a whole pumpkin in a plastic bag in the microwave. The skin will come off easily once cooked and the pumpkin retains its flavour better this way.

Roasted pumpkin seeds

Wash the seeds and leave to dry on a paper towel. Grease a baking tray well with oil or butter. Put the pumpkin seeds on the tray in a single layer and brush with a little oil before baking at 150 °C until light brown.

SPINACH

- Flavour spinach with lemon juice and a pinch of nutmeg.
- Add cubes of bacon to spinach while cooking.
- Stir-fry spinach in olive oil and season with garlic.

SWEET POTATO

Sweet treat

If you do not have yellow sugar to add to sweet potatoes, mix a little turmeric with white sugar.

How to store sweet potatoes

To prevent the cut side of a sweet potato going blue, spread it with margarine before storing.

Sticky ring

Some oil in the water when cooking sweet potatoes will prevent a sticky ring forming around the pot, which is difficult to remove.

TOMATOES

How to peel tomatoes

- Cover tomatoes in boiling water and leave to stand for a minute before plunging into cold water. The skin will burst, making it easy to peel off.
- You can also place tomatoes on a paper towel in the microwave and cook on full power for 10–15 seconds. Leave to cool and then remove the skins.

Green tomatoes

Ripen green tomatoes in a brown paper bag in the fridge.

Overripe tomatoes

If tomatoes are too soft for a salad, put them in a bowl of cold salted water for a few minutes to firm up.

Freezing

- Tomatoes can be frozen whole. Hold a frozen tomato under a running tap for 30 seconds and it will peel easily.
- Make your own tomato sauce for pasta and freeze it in sachets.
- You can also freeze tomato purée in an ice tray and use the cubes in soups and drinks.

Whole tomato slices

Dip sliced tomato into flour to stop it breaking up when fried.

Sun-dried tomatoes

Soak sun-dried tomatoes in a liquid such as water, wine or vegetable stock before use. If you are not going to use them immediately, place them in a bottle with olive oil and store in the fridge. Add a garlic clove for extra flavour.

If tomatoes are too soft for a salad, put them in a bowl of cold salted water for a few minutes to firm up.

7.3 HERBS AND SPICES

Herbal salt

Make your own blend of dried, ground herbs from your garden, and mix with salt. Use this blend instead of pure salt, thereby reducing your salt consumption.

Fresh rosemary salt

Mix half a cup of sea salt with two teaspoons fresh rosemary leaves. Lavender, thyme or grated lemon rind could be used instead of rosemary. Let your taste be your guide.

Aniseed

- Aniseed can be used whole or in powdered form. Aniseed is a strong flavour that tends to dominate and should be used in small quantities.
- Liven up apple purée by cooking half a teaspoon aniseed (the seeds) with the apples.

Cinnamon

- Cinnamon is popular in baking and can also be used in Middle Eastern meat dishes in combination with cloves, nutmeg and aniseed.
- A pinch of cinnamon will liven up cocoa, hot chocolate, coffee and tea.

Seasoning for lamb chops

To bring out the flavour of lamb chops, use this spice mix: combine a little white pepper, a pinch of finely ground cloves, half a handful of ground coriander and salt to taste.

Mint

Dip mint leaves in vinegar before making mint sauce or jelly. This keeps the leaves beautifully green.

Cloves

- This hot toddy is perfect for winter evenings or when you're nursing a cold: heat a cup of red wine with one clove and a few pieces of orange rind. Stir in two teaspoons of honey before serving.

- Make savoury rice by putting a few cloves, a garlic clove or two and the peel of half a lemon into a muslin bag; tie it and cook it along with the rice.

To bring out the flavour of lamb chops, use this spice mix: Combine a little pepper, a pinch of ground cloves, half a handful of ground coriander and salt to taste.

PARSLEY

Chopped parsley

- Rinse parsley in hot water first and it will be easier to chop finely.
- Freeze leftover parsley in an ice tray.

Use scissors

When you are in a hurry, it is easier to snip parsley directly into the dish using a pair of scissors. The same applies to chives and other herbs.

Dried parsley

Dry fresh parsley in a moderate oven with the door ajar. Store in an airtight container.

7.4 FRUIT

APPLES

Easy peeling

Plunge apples into boiling water for a few seconds to make them easier to peel.

Shiny apples

Brush a little mild salad dressing made with oil and vinegar over apples before baking to give them an even colour.

Prevent bursting

Whole apples that are baked in the oven have a tendency to burst. Prevent this by peeling a small strip off each one before baking.

Dried apples

Apples last a long time if they are dried. Cut each apple into quarters and remove the core and pips. Brush with lemon juice and dry in the sun or in the oven on a low temperature.

Prevent discolouration

Adding a dash of lemon juice to the water will stop apples discolouring as they cook.

Toffee apples

If the syrup into which you dip the apples goes hard too quickly, put it in the fridge for a few minutes, then reheat slowly until it is liquid again.

Toffee grapes

Thread grapes onto a kebab stick and dip in syrup used to make toffee apples.

Avocado pear

Sprinkle lemon juice on avocado cubes for a salad to stop them going brown.

- An avocado can also be dipped in boiling water for a few seconds before peeling to help prevent discolouration.
- Why not eat your avo the Brazilian way and sprinkle it with sugar?

Grapefruit

Sprinkle salt over grapefruit to improve the taste.

Pawpaw

- Pawpaw is a versatile fruit that should not be limited to fruit salad.
- Thread pieces of the fruit onto kebab sticks along with meat and cook on the braai.
- Green pawpaw and pork ribs make a delicious soup, and you can cook green pawpaw on its own and serve it like pumpkin.

BANANAS

Green bananas

Ripen green bananas quickly by wrapping them in a damp cloth and storing in a brown paper bag.

Freezing bananas

- Fry banana slices in a little butter. Then freeze to use later with dishes such as curries.
- You can also freeze mashed banana that has been sprinkled with lemon juice.
- Overripe bananas can be frozen whole for use in baking later. When needed, defrost, peel and mash with a fork.

Pineapple

Fresh pineapple is not suitable for dishes made with gelatine because it contains the enzyme bromelin that will prevent the gelatine from setting. If you want to make a dessert or jelly with pineapple, use canned pineapple or cook the pieces of fruit in a little water first. Heating destroys the enzyme. The same applies to pawpaws, which contain the enzyme papain.

Rhubarb

When cooking rhubarb, keep the lid on the pot to retain the lovely red colour. Dissolve a packet of red jelly powder in the liquid in which the rhubarb is cooked to make it even tastier.

Cleaning rhubarb

Soaking rhubarb in iced water for 10 minutes makes it easier to clean.

Always make sure that the equipment and bottles used to make and store jam or marmalade are sterilised before use.

CITRUS FRUIT

Warm it up

To extract more juice from citrus fruit, heat the fruit for 10 minutes in boiling water before squeezing. Heating it briefly in the microwave will have the same effect.

Lemon halves

Keep lemon halves fresher for longer by brushing egg white on the cut end.

How to store citrus fruit

Citrus fruit can last for up to a month when wrapped in tissue paper and then packed in sawdust.

Citrus zest

Always grate the peel of a lemon or orange before squeezing or eating the fruit. Then mix the zest with sugar and store in an airtight container in the fridge. The zest lends a subtle but delicious flavour to baked puddings, vanilla sponge and home-made chocolates.

Flavoured olive oil

- Make lemon olive oil by pressing three cloves into a few lemons and packing the lemons into a glass jar. Fill the jar with olive oil and store in a cool, dark place.
- Instead of lemons, use garlic, peppercorns and a sprig of fresh rosemary.

Figs

Rub your arms and hands generously with butter before picking or peeling figs. The butter will protect you from the fine hairs that can cause an unpleasant itch.

DRIED FRUIT

Soft fruit for breakfast

Soak dried fruit overnight in boiling water, a rooibos tea bag, one stick cinnamon, dried naartjie peel or cloves. Enjoy the flavoured fruit in the morning for breakfast.

Keep mites away

Place a small dish of brandy among a large store of dried fruit to keep the mites away. Replace the brandy when it evaporates.

Storing dried fruit

Dried fruit can be stored in a pillowcase that has been dipped in a very strong salt solution beforehand.

That sinking feeling

Heat dried fruit in the oven for a few minutes and sprinkle it with flour before adding it to batter. This will stop the fruit sinking to the bottom.

Crystallised fruit

Using a wet knife makes crystallised fruit easier to cut.

JAM

Burnt jam

Drop a few clean marbles into the bottom of the pot when making jam to prevent it burning and sticking to the bottom.

Crystallised jam

Add 5 ml glycerine per jar of jam to the mixture just before the end of the cooking time to prevent jam crystallising later.

Cleaner than clean

Always make sure that the equipment and bottles used to make and store jam or marmalade are sterilised before use.

Start small

If you are a novice at jam-making but still want to produce a great product, it is better to start with a small quantity. Cook the amount of fruit you need to make approximately four litres of jam. This will enable you to regulate the temperature and there is less chance of the fruit being cooked to mush. Your jam will also not go too dark.

Extra jam

Make 500 g more jam by adding a packet of jelly dissolved in 250 ml water. Add the jelly mixture to the boiling jam and cook them well together.

Remove foam

Keep skimming the foam off the boiling jam to ensure a clear finished product.

Lemons for pectin

Add extra lemon juice to jam that will not set as a result of the fruit having a low pectin content.

Get rid of pips

Add 12,5 ml vinegar to grape jam just before it is due to come off the stove. Then boil the jam rapidly and the pips will float to the surface, allowing you to skim them off with a spoon.

Runny honey

If honey has become too thick to pour, stand the jar in boiling water or place it in the microwave on medium power for 10 seconds.

Dark and light honey

There are literally hundreds of different types of honey. Use this rule of thumb to help you choose: the darker the honey, the stronger the flavour.

7.5 BAKING

Get dough to rise

Encourage bread dough to rise rapidly by wrapping the pan containing the dough securely in a plastic bag together with a bowl of hot water.

Dough that rises too fast

If bread dough is rising too quickly and the oven is not quite ready, place the dough in the fridge for a while.

Smarten up microwave bread

Give bread baked in the microwave a lovely golden colour by brushing it with a beaten egg or some soy sauce. You could also sprinkle the dough with cheese or poppy seeds.

Shoebox loaf

Bake bread in a small shoebox in the microwave. Afterwards you can throw the box away and save on the washing up.

Uses for stale bread

- Make breadcrumbs and dry them by microwaving 250 ml crumbs on 100% power for five minutes. You can also make breadcrumbs in an oven that is cooling after making another dish.
- Home-made croutons are tasty and easy to make: cut stale bread into cubes and dry in the oven like rusks. Olive oil sprinkled over the croutons adds to the flavour.
- To revive slightly stale bread, sprinkle with water or milk and bake in a 120 °C oven for approximately 30 minutes.
- Make a bread pudding.
- Feed stale bread to the earthworms, even if it has gone a bit mouldy.

If your oven bakes unevenly, cover the bottom oven rack with tinfoil to reflect and distribute the heat more evenly.

Brown the crust

Bake pies and tarts on a metal tray so that the bottom of the crust also turns brown and crisp.

Perfect pastry

- Add a little lemon juice to the water when making pastry.
- To seal the sides of pastry, brush on some prepared gelatine and press to seal. Egg white or milk applied using your fingers also works well.

Air vent

Stick a piece of macaroni through the middle of a pastry lid to allow steam to escape during baking. This helps prevent gravy leaking out the sides. You could also use an old-fashioned pie vent.

Crisp crust

Brush beaten egg white on the inside of a pastry casing before spooning in the filling. This will keep the crust beautifully crisp.

Improvised baking tray

Cover an oven rack in tinfoil and use it as a tray for baking biscuits, saving on the washing up.

Uneven baking

If your oven bakes unevenly, cover the bottom oven rack with tinfoil to reflect and distribute the heat more evenly.

Difficult dough

When dough keeps breaking as you roll it out, place it between two sheets of wax paper and then roll it out.

Prevent cracks

Add a sheet of unflavoured gelatine to the batter to prevent cracks in the top of a cake.

Lemon makes it light

Adding a teaspoon of lemon juice to the sugar and butter while you cream them will make the cake lovely and light.

Cream butter well

The longer and lighter you cream the butter before adding the sugar, the better the cake will rise. Soften hard butter by microwaving it for a few seconds.

Doubly delicious chocolate cake

- Add a teaspoon of vinegar to chocolate cake batter before adding the bicarbonate of soda.
- A tablespoon of raspberry or plum jam added to the batter will enhance the flavour.
- Replace the milk in a chocolate-cake recipe with cold coffee.

Moist fruitcake

Place a pan of boiling water in the bottom of the oven when baking a moist fruitcake. The water will produce steam that keeps the cake moist. Add more boiling water if it evaporates.

Decorating tips

- Do not attempt to decorate a cake before it is completely cold.
- Sprinkle the cake lightly with caster sugar before you start icing.
- To prevent the cake absorbing the icing or filling, spread a little butter on the layers before icing.

Hairdryer for shine

Once you have decorated the cake, use a hairdryer to melt the icing slightly and obtain a smooth, shiny surface. The same effect can be obtained using a warm spatula.

Flawless icing

Add a pinch of bicarbonate of soda to the icing sugar when making fondant icing to stop the icing cracking.

Smooth frosting

Mix a heaped tablespoon of cornflour into each cup of icing sugar to ensure a smooth frosting.

Koeksisters keep well in the freezer for a long time.

Coconut on cake

To prevent coconut drawing moisture out of a cake, soak the coconut in milk first and drain well before sprinkling on the cake.

Glacé icing

Make glacé icing for petits fours using hot water or brandy to give the finished product a professional-looking sheen.

Leftover cake

Turn leftover cake into trifle by layering it in a bowl along with jelly, custard and canned fruit.

Ring tin

If you do not have a ring baking tin, fashion one by placing an ovenproof glass or cup in the middle of an ordinary round tin. Grease the cup with oil and hold it in place while pouring in the batter to ensure it does not move.

Buttermilk for baking

To make baked goods such as scones, pancakes and flapjacks as light as a feather, replace the milk and water with buttermilk.

Light pancakes

Use soda water instead of tap water in pancake batter to make it lighter.

Perfect pancakes

Add 5 ml brandy to every litre of pancake batter to prevent the pancakes going tough.

Allow to rest

It is important to leave pancake and flapjack batter to rest for 10 to 15 minutes before cooking them.

Perfect biscuits

- Keep biscuit dough as cold as possible. It if gets too warm the biscuits will be doughy.
- Do not try to roll out all the dough at the same time.
- If you work biscuit dough too much, it becomes tough when baked.
- Dip the cookie cutter into flour before cutting out biscuits so that it does not stick to the dough.
- Swap the baking trays halfway through the baking time so that all the biscuits bake evenly.

Make koeksisters shine

Add a knife-point of cream of tartar to the syrup to make koeksisters lovely and shiny.

Freeze koeksisters

Koeksisters keep well in the freezer for a long time, and can also be eaten straight from the freezer because the syrup does not freeze.

Custard powder for koeksisters

Sprinkle custard powder on the surface on which you plait koeksisters. This will give the koeksisters a lovely colour and the oil will spatter less.

7.6 EGGS

Warning

Because of the risk of salmonella infection, pregnant women, young children and the elderly should avoid raw egg and products made with raw egg, unless the source of the eggs is impeccable. Salmonella is found mainly in eggs that are mass-produced.

Cracked egg

If an egg has cracked in the box, cover the crack with sticky tape and it should not spread further when boiling.

Prick the shell

If you want to place an ice-cold egg in boiling water without it cracking, prick a hole in the rounded end of the egg first. The hole allows air in the sac to escape and prevents the shell from cracking.

How to save egg yolks

- Place the yolk in a saucer and cover it with half an egg shell before putting it in the fridge.
- Make a small hole in the shell and allow the white to run out. Store the yolk in the shell in the fridge.
- Leftover egg yolks can also be covered with water and stored in an airtight container in the fridge.
- Break the egg into a narrow funnel. The white will run through leaving the whole yolk behind.

Keep stirring

Stir eggs while they boil to keep the yolk in the middle, especially if you intend making stuffed eggs.

Easy peeling

Add a dash of vinegar to the water when boiling eggs to make them easier to peel. Also plunge the cooked eggs into ice-cold water immediately.

Separate an egg by hand

Your hand is the perfect egg separator: allow the white to run through your fingers while the yolk remains behind.

Keep eggs longer: Seal with oil

To keep raw eggs for longer, seal the shells using a little olive or sunflower oil. Rub the shells lightly with the oil and put the eggs back in the box in which you bought them. Store in the fridge. Turn the egg box twice a week to keep the yolks in the middle.

Home-made mayonnaise

1. Mix one egg yolk, half a teaspoon garlic, one tablespoon lemon juice and one teaspoon mustard powder in a food processor, or use a whisk or hand beater.
2. Slowly add three-quarters of a cup of olive oil to the mixture while continuing to process or whisk until a thick emulsion forms.
3. Season with salt and pepper to taste.

Stop mayonnaise separating

- Home-made mayonnaise tends to separate easily. To emulsify the mixture again, add a tablespoon of boiling water to the separated mayonnaise, drop by drop, while beating continuously.
- Make mayonnaise wonderfully light by folding in a beaten egg white just before serving.

Mayonnaise versus aïoli

Although aïoli and mayonnaise are prepared in the same way, aïoli is traditionally made without egg and contains only garlic, oil and lemon juice. However, an egg yolk helps the mixture form an emulsion quicker. Mayonnaise, on the other hand, is traditionally made using only egg yolks, oil and salt and pepper.

Beating egg whites

- Egg whites will not become stiff if there is any egg yolk in the bowl.
- Also ensure that the bowl and beater are free of grease.
- If the whites will not form peaks, add a dash of lemon juice or a pinch of salt.
- Egg whites at room temperature can be beaten to a bigger volume than if the whites are cold.

Yolk in the egg whites
If some egg yolk gets into the whites, you can rescue the situation with a cloth. Wet a corner of the cloth with water and dip the edge into the egg white. The yolk will be attracted to the cloth and you can lift it out.

Keep egg whites stiff
To keep egg whites stiff for longer, beat in a quarter of a teaspoon of cream of tartar to every two egg whites.

Marvellous meringues
The secret to getting a meringue mixture to hold good peaks is to add the caster sugar to the whisked egg whites slowly, a little at a time. Use icing sugar instead of caster sugar for even stiffer peaks.

Off or not?
Eggs that float are no longer fresh; fresh eggs will always sink. If you are in any doubt, break the egg into a separate container to test it.

Cooking for a crowd
Cook a number of eggs at a time in a muffin pan. Grease the pan well, crack an egg into each hollow and put the pan in the oven at 160 °C until the eggs are cooked to your liking.

Cooked or not?
Sort hard-boiled eggs from raw ones by spinning them on the table. The hard-boiled ones will spin for longer.

Fluffy omelettes
Add a pinch of baking powder for every two eggs when making omelettes and they will turn out wonderfully light and fluffy.

7.7 DAIRY PRODUCTS

Cream butter by using a bowl that has been dipped in boiling water first.

MILK

Well sealed

Make sure milk bottles are well sealed in the fridge because milk tends to absorb odours.

Freezing milk

The nutritional value of milk that has been frozen remains unchanged, but the texture may differ slightly once defrosted.

Butter fat

The lower the percentage of butter fat in the milk, the easier it is for the cream to separate from the milk.

Skimmed milk

Skimmed milk contains proportionally more calcium than full-cream milk because calcium is present in the water of milk and not in the butter fat. Skimmed milk contains less butter fat and therefore more calcium per portion.

Stop milk boiling over

To prevent milk boiling over, rub some butter around the rim or on the bottom of the saucepan.

CREAM

Long-lasting whipped cream

To get whipped cream to hold its shape for longer, add one teaspoon of gelatine dissolved in two tablespoons of water to the cream just before you finish whipping it.

Flavoured cream

- Whip two tablespoons of cocoa and two tablespoons of sugar with cream to make chocolate cream.
- Two tablespoons of instant coffee granules and two tablespoons of sugar give cream a mocha flavour.
- Add a tablespoon of your favourite liqueur for an extra-special cream.

Butter

Remember: beating cream for too long produces butter.

Creaming butter

Make it easier to cream butter by using a bowl that has been dipped in boiling water first.

CHEESE

Dried-out cheese

Rescue dried-out cheese by leaving it in salt water for while.

How to freeze cheese

- Hard or semi-hard cheese freezes well. Wipe the cut end with a small amount of butter, wrap in clingfilm and place in a freezer bag.
- Allow frozen cheese to defrost slowly in the fridge. Cheese may have a crumbly texture once thawed.
- Do not freeze soft cheese because the texture changes substantially after freezing.

Make your own cheese board

Select approximately five different cheeses, with flavours ranging from neutral to sharp. Also choose cheeses with different textures and colours. Serve with dried fruit and bread or crackers.

7.8 HASSLE-FREE FREEZING

Remember to remember

Keep a list of everything in your freezer and cross out items as you remove them.

Spoons of cream

Place spoonfuls of whipped cream on wax paper, put in an airtight container and freeze. These spoonfuls of cream are perfect for adding to soups and desserts.

Spoons of pesto

Spoonfuls of pesto can also be frozen for a short time. Add the frozen pesto to dishes during cooking.

Edible flowers

Place edible flowers or mint leaves in an ice tray and fill with water. Freeze and serve in drinks or to garnish cold soup.

Leftover wine

Freeze leftover wine in ice trays to use later in cooking.

Lemon juice

Freeze fresh lemon juice in ice trays. Frozen juice comes in handy when fresh citrus fruit is scarce.

Keep frozen meat separate

Use clingfilm to cover a large tray that fits into the freezer. Arrange a single layer of meat cuts on the tray and cover with clingfilm, ensuring that the meat is completely covered. Repeat with more layers, then freeze. Once frozen, the cuts will be separate and then you can package them for freezing in portions. Mark clearly and return to the freezer.

Pretty ice

Use the plastic containers in which chocolate truffles or bonbons are packaged to make ice. (These containers often have interesting patterns.) Freeze a cherry, an edible flower or a mint leaf in the ice. Such containers are also suitable for making chocolates or handmade soap.

Frozen bags

When storing frozen food in plastic bags in the freezer, it is a good idea to spray the outside of the bags with cooking spray to prevent them sticking together.

Different colours

Use different-coloured freezer bags for different types of meat or food you want to freeze. This makes finding what you are looking for in the freezer a whole lot easier.

Microwave-safe plastic

Package food that you intend defrosting or reheating in the microwave, in microwave-safe containers.

Smaller portions

Freeze food in smaller portions, rather than larger ones, because they freeze faster and are easier to defrost.

Cooldrink lollies

Freeze cooldrink in ice trays or in plastic ice-lolly makers for a delicious treat on a hot day.

Berries and pineapple

Freeze chopped pineapple and a variety of berries to reduce the time it takes to make a smoothie in the morning.

Plastic bottles

Freeze soups or stews in plastic bottles and milk containers, and save a great deal of space in your freezer.

Bags of water

Wash out the empty bag from a boxed wine, then remove the tap and wash it well too. Fill the bag with water, replace the tap and freeze. It is perfect for ensuring ice-cold drinking water on the beach or on a picnic on a hot day.

Freeze fresh lemon juice in ice trays. Frozen juice comes in handy when fresh citrus fruit is scarce.

Freeze food scraps

- During the summer, freeze perishable food scraps and refuse in plastic bags, and place in the bin just before the refuse is removed. This prevents nasty smells and pests in your municipal bin.
- Fruit and vegetable peels and scraps can be wrapped in a couple of sheets of newspaper and buried in the garden. Dig a hole just big enough for the parcel, but deep enough to keep it out of reach of inquisitive dogs.

7.9 USEFUL SUBSTITUTES

Buttermilk

Plain or Bulgarian yoghurt can be used instead of buttermilk.

Cornflour

Use ordinary flour if you do not have cornflour in the house, but double the quantity.

A cup of flour

Can be replaced with one cup of fine breadcrumbs.

Food colouring

Use neat, coloured cordials to colour icing sugar.

Eggs in baking

- To replace eggs, mix two tablespoons water with one tablespoon cooking oil and two teaspoons baking powder. Mix well before use.
- Alternatively, use 10 ml gelatine dissolved in 15 ml hot water.
- Tofu is also a suitable replacement because it takes on the flavour of the dish you are using it in. A quarter of a cup of puréed silken tofu is equivalent to one egg and it can be used in cakes, puddings and smoothies.

Caster sugar

Make your own caster sugar by putting ordinary sugar into a plastic bag and rolling it fine with a rolling pin.

Coconut milk

Make your own coconut milk by combining a cup of desiccated coconut with a cup of hot milk and leaving it to stand for an hour. Use as is or strain and use only the milk.

Alcohol substitutes

- *Amaretto:* Use half a teaspoon almond essence for every two tablespoons Amaretto.

- *Apple brandy:* Use apple juice or unsweetened apple concentrate.
- *Beer:* Use chicken stock, ginger ale or non-alcoholic beer.
- *Bourbon or whiskey:* Replace with two teaspoons vanilla essence.
- *Brandy:* Two teaspoons brandy essence and as much fruit juice as the amount of brandy called for in the recipe.
- *Champagne/sparkling wine:* Ginger ale, sparkling apple juice or sparkling white grape juice.
- *Cherry liqueur:* The syrup from a tin of cherries.
- *Coffee liqueur:* To replace two tablespoons coffee liqueur, mix one teaspoon chocolate syrup with one teaspoon instant coffee granules.
- *Cognac:* Use apple juice.
- *Cointreau and Grand Marnier:* Replace two tablespoons Cointreau or Grand Marnier with two tablespoons orange juice and half a teaspoon orange essence.
- *Kirschwasser (Kirsch):* Use black cherry juice, apple juice or raspberry juice.
- *Red wine:* Add a tablespoon of lemon juice or vinegar to every 25 ml currant jelly, cranberry sauce or tomato juice.
- *Vodka:* Mix white grape juice or apple juice with lime juice.
- *White wine:* Use alcohol-free wine or add a tablespoon of vinegar to white grape juice, apple juice or chicken stock.

Baking powder

Make your own baking powder by sifting together 30 ml cream of tartar, 15 ml bicarbonate of soda and 10 ml cornflour a few times.

Self-raising flour

You can make your own self-raising flour by sifting together 500 ml plain flour, 5 ml bicarbonate of soda and 10 ml cream of tartar.

Baking chocolate

Combine 45 ml cocoa and 10 ml butter, and sweeten to taste. Instant chocolate milk powder can be used instead of cocoa powder. Chocolate spread is also a suitable replacement.

Butter or margarine
This can be replaced with sunflower oil. Approximately 15 ml butter or margarine is equal to 12,5 ml oil.

Chutney
Mix Worcestershire sauce with apricot jam to make a substitute for chutney.

Tomato sauce
Combine 125 ml sugar, two tablespoons vinegar and a 250 ml tin of tomato purée.

7.10 GENERAL TIPS

Fresh bread

Pop an apple or a peeled potato into the bread bin to keep bread fresh for longer.

Wrinkled nuts

Soak nuts that have become wrinkled in water to allow them to swell up again.

Dried-out mustard

- Prevent mustard drying out by sprinkling a little salt on top. A slice of lemon on top will do the same thing.
- If mustard has already dried out, you can save it by stirring through a small spoonful of sugar and a little vinegar.

Gelatine

Gelatine will dissolve faster if you soak it in cold water first before adding the hot water.

Salty stock

- Rescue stock that is too salty by adding a teaspoon of sugar.
- Cook a chopped-up potato along with the stock to absorb some of the salt.

Pizza cutter

A pizza cutter is useful for cutting almost any food quickly – from fudge and pancakes to chicken strips.

Grapefruit spoon

Use a grapefruit spoon to remove seeds from chillies, gem squash and tomatoes.

Vegetable peeler

Use a vegetable peeler to make chocolate curls and to cut larger pieces of lemon and orange zest.

Bamboo for garlic

Store garlic and onions in a Chinese bamboo steamer.

Notes

Notes

the HOUSE inside & out 8

Golden rule for a happy home

"A house should be clean enough to be healthy and dirty enough to be happy."

Anonymous

8.1 WINDOWS

Keep dry

Stop your arms getting wet while washing windows by making thick arm bands for your wrists from foam rubber.

Sparkling clean

- Quarter an onion and drop it skin and all into the window-washing water, which should be hot. This will help prevent streaks on the windows.
- You can polish windows with newspaper or an old stocking to prevent streaks.

Find those streaks

Wash the outside of windows from left to right and the inside from top to bottom, and you will easily be able to spot where the streaks are.

Fly deposits

Wash fly droppings (tiny black dots) off windows using a sponge and cold tea. Tea contains an acid that keeps flies away.

Salt and vinegar

Wash windows with salt or vinegar water to make them sparkle.

Filthy windows

Tackle very dirty windows with a solution of 45 ml white vinegar, 15 ml bleach and five litres boiling water.

Copper window fasteners

Clean copper window fasteners with steel wool dipped first in water and then in tartaric acid. Leave to stand for a while and then polish with a damp cloth.

Fold up fragile, sun-damaged curtains before washing gently in salt water to prevent further damage.

Get it straight

Position a curtain rail parallel to the window frame and the ceiling line, rather than using a spirit level because ceilings and window frames are often not level.

Choose the right rail

Curtain rails come in different lengths and weights and it is therefore important to choose the right rail for the type of fabric. The rail must be at least 30 cm longer than the width of the window.

Curtain length

Curtains can be any length, but remember that ceiling-to-floor drops make the ceiling look higher. Hang short curtains closer to the window. Drops that billow onto the floor can be attractive, but you need plenty of space to carry off this look.

Fragile curtains

Fold up fragile, sun-damaged curtains before washing gently in salt water to prevent further damage.

Velvet drapes

To refresh velvet curtains, hang them over a steaming bath. Then brush against the nap using a stiff brush.

Curtain pullers

Help keep your curtains clean by installing curtain pullers. To make your own, buy metre-long or longer wooden dowels. Paint the dowels and insert a hook at one end. Attach additional curtain hooks to the curtain rail so that you can hook a puller in front of the lead ring on each drop.

Canvas blinds

Wash roller blinds in lukewarm water with a little washing powder. Rinse well in cold water and allow to dry completely before reinstalling.

Blind cords that last

The cords on blinds will last longer if you rub them with a little petroleum jelly.

8.2 LAMPS AND LIGHTS

Safety first

- Unplug lamps and switch off ceiling lights at the light switch before you start cleaning them.
- Never touch a switch or a light that is on while your hands are wet.

Taking lamps apart

Always ensure that you know how to put a light fitting back together again before taking it apart to clean.

Fabric lampshades

Vacuum fabric lampshades gently from time to time to remove dust, as most fabric shades are not washable.

Glass and metal lampshades

Dust with a feather duster or normal duster.

Plastic lampshades

Wash in fairly hot water and a small amount of dishwashing liquid.

Paper lampshades

Dust regularly and replace if the shade becomes discoloured.

Nylon and rayon lampshades

Dip repeatedly in hot, soapy water. Rinse in hot water and dry quickly.

Bulbs

Ensure that a bulb is cold before touching it, and remove it carefully and gently.

8.3 FURNITURE

Oak furniture

To keep oak furniture gleaming like new, wash with a little warm beer and then polish with a dry cloth.

Water marks

Remove water marks from wood by dipping a cork into a mixture of cigarette ash (or salt) and cooking oil and then gently wiping it over the mark. Keep rubbing until a grey slurry forms. Wipe it off and the mark should be gone. Warning: this method could damage the patina of wooden furniture and leave a lighter patch.

Pet hair

Remove hair shed by your cat or dog by putting on a damp rubber glove and rubbing the affected area. The hair should roll up into a ball, which can be removed easily.

Marks on leather

Make a grease mark on leather furniture less obvious by sprinkling baby powder on it. Leave for a few days and then clean with a vacuum cleaner.

Beautify leather furniture

Refresh leather furniture every now and then by rubbing in a mixture of equal quantities of olive oil and vinegar.

Upholstered furniture

Clean upholstered furniture with a damp cloth and a white vinegar and water mixture.

Mould on furniture

Remove mould from furniture by rubbing it with a cloth dipped in paraffin.

Cane furniture

Wash cane and rattan furniture with water and non-alkaline soap.

8.4 FLOORS AND WALLS

Natural stone

Natural stone contains a lot of lime. Never clean natural stone floors with anything containing an acid, such as vinegar or lemon.

Marble

Clean marble with a little methylated spirits on a dry cloth.

Felt-tipped pen

Remove marks from a felt-tipped pen from smooth surfaces by spraying with a mixture of methylated spirits and tartaric acid.

Vacuum wallpaper

- Tie a cloth around the end of vacuum-cleaner hose and vacuum the wallpaper.
- Washable wallpaper can be washed using lukewarm water and a small amount of dishwashing liquid.

Pen marks on wallpaper

Remove pen marks from wallpaper by first dampening the area and then spraying it with hairspray. Leave to soak in for a while before wiping with a dry cloth.

Accidents on the carpet

- If the spill has just happened, remove as much as possible and treat the mark with soda water. The soiling will bubble out. Then dab lightly to dry using a dry cloth. (Also see the stain-removal tips, pages 26–32.)
- Marks can also be dabbed repeatedly with hot water to get them clean. Do not soak in hot water, which will only worsen the stain.

Cat urine

To rid a carpet of the smell of cat urine, wash the area with water first and then with a solution of hot water and dishwashing liquid. Press with a towel to dry. Then mix half a cup of white vinegar with hot water and use it to wash the spot thoroughly. Once it is clean, try to absorb as much of the moisture as possible using paper towels. Keep replacing the paper until the area is dry.

Dirty marks on cowhide

Using hot water and dishwashing liquid, rub the spot gently with a sponge until clean. Dab the moisture immediately using a dry cloth. Be careful not to wet the skin, or it will curl up when it dries again.

Get loose rugs to lie flat

- If you have a loose rug that keeps curling up at the edges, get it to lie flat by painting the bottom with varnish.
- Small mats can also be rinsed in or sponged with a solution of laundry starch and water.

Candle wax on a wooden floor

Carefully scrape off the wax in the direction of the grain of the wood, then rub the area clean with eucalyptus oil.

Whitewashing wooden floors

Scrub a wooden floor with a stiff brush, lime and coarse sand to obtain a white-washed effect.

Rubber marks

Remove marks on wooden floors from rubber shoe soles using an eraser.

No more dull laminated floors

Brighten dull laminated floors by adding a little dishwasher rinse aid to the soapy water when washing them.

Bamboo and rush matting

Vacuum the mats regularly and wash twice a year using a small amount of salt water.

Coir mats and carpets

Dampen coir mats and carpets from time to time to keep them supple. Brush the mat with water in which a small amount of washing soda has been dissolved.

Cleaning the fireplace

Lay plenty of newspaper in front of the fireplace and then saturate the paper with water using a spray bottle. Scrape out the ash and coals onto the wet newspaper, which will stop the ash from flying about. Fold up the newspaper carefully and throw away.

Absorb stale smells

Place a few dishes of vinegar in strategic places in the living area to get rid of stale smells from a party. Placing dishes of bicarbonate of soda in your home before a party absorbs cigarette smoke and fumes.

The scent of cinnamon

Simmer cinnamon sticks, orange peel and cloves in a pot of water on the stove and the scent will permeate your entire home.

8.5 COPPER AND SILVERWARE

Keep the shine

Stop shiny copper from tarnishing by wiping it with olive oil and polishing it to a shine.

Polish copper

Copper is easy to polish using a paste of vinegar and salt.

Tomato fix

Rub tomato purée on copper that has gone black and leave it on overnight. Rinse with warm water and then polish using copper polish or a mixture of milk and a little salt.

Lasting shine

Keep copper bright for longer by spraying it with hairspray.

Silverware

Silver tarnishes quickly in a humid, salty environment. Wash as soon as possible after use in hot soapy water, rinse in hot water and dry immediately. Place a block of camphor in the cutlery drawer to stop silver cutlery tarnishing again quickly.

Silver polish

Apply silver polish with a soft cloth and use an old toothbrush to reach the crevices. Then rub the silver clean using up-and-down movements. Polish with a soft cloth or chamois and wash it again to remove polish residue, which can cause silver to tarnish again quickly. Dry thoroughly.

Rub tomato purée on copper that has gone black and leave it on overnight. Rinse with warm water and then polish using copper polish or a mixture of milk and a little salt.

Dip a pipe cleaner in silver polish and work it between the prongs of silver forks to clean them properly.

Natural silver polish

Polish silver with a paste made from bicarbonate of soda and water. Leave the paste on stubborn marks for an hour or more. Wash and dry with a soft cloth.

Pipe cleaner

Dip a pipe cleaner in silver polish and work it between the prongs of silver forks to clean them properly.

Marks on silver

- Use a raw potato to remove marks on silverware with ease.
- You could also try cigarette ash.
- Wash silverware in a solution of 12,5 ml borax and two cups of water to keep it shiny.

Candle wax in candlesticks

- Soak glass, silver, metal and china candlesticks in very hot water with a little dishwashing liquid. Once the wax is soft, carefully remove it. Make sure you remove all the wax from the sink before letting the water out.
- In summer, place the candlesticks in the hot sun to melt the wax.
- Melt the wax using a hairdryer and remove it once it has softened.
- Alternatively, put the candlestick in the freezer to harden the wax, making it easier to remove.

Notes

ELECTRONIC goods 9

Read the manual

Always consult the manual before attempting to clean electronic goods and appliances.

General computer-cleaning tips

- Switch off the computer before you start cleaning.
- Do not spray any liquids on computer parts. Rather spray them onto a cloth and then wipe the computer with the cloth.
- Use a vacuum cleaner to clean the outside of the computer, but do not vacuum inside a computer because this causes static electricity that could damage the computer's memory. Rather blow away the dust through pursed lips.
- When cleaning the back of a computer, take care not to pull out any plugs.
- Clean the fan on a laptop computer by holding it gently and blowing air onto it through pursed lips.
- Never eat or drink over a computer.

Cleaning older-generation glass monitors

A computer monitor with a glass screen can be cleaned using ordinary window or glass cleaner. Remember not to leave anything lying on the ventilation grille on top of the monitor.

Mouse and mouse pad

To ensure optimum functioning, clean the mouse and mouse pad as well. If the mouse is an older type with a ball inside, remove the ball and clean it too.

Printers and scanners

Wipe printers and scanners carefully using a damp cloth. The glass surface of the scanner can be cleaned with window cleaner.

Compact discs

- Before you buy a compact-disc cleaning kit, try the following: use a non-static cloth, isopropyl alcohol (C_3H_8O), plain dishwashing liquid and distilled water. An old T-shirt or handkerchief is a useful replacement for a non-static cloth.
- Wet the cloth and wipe the compact disc clean from the middle to the edge. Do not clean in a circle around the disc. Repeat, but this time add a small amount of soap to the water. Dry the disc well. Using another clean cloth dipped in alcohol this time, wipe the compact disc again. The alcohol evaporates quickly so you do not need to dry it.

- Do not use hydrogen peroxide, window cleaner or any type of metal polish on compact discs.

Cleaning a compact disc player

1. First make sure there is no disc in the player. Then open the tray of the player and unplug the player at the wall. The tray will remain open.
2. Unscrew the cover and keep the screws in a safe place. Spray WD-40 onto a cotton bud and clean the rails of the disc player.
3. Dip a clean cotton bud into surgical spirits and use it to clean the lens of the laser.
4. Screw the cover in position again and turn the player on without a disc in it to allow the laser to slide back into place.

- Warning: video gaming equipment cannot be cleaned in this way.

Cleaning LCD screens on computers, TV sets, laptops and palmtops

- LCD screens are not made of glass and must therefore be cleaned extra carefully. Do not spray water or a cleaning material directly onto the screen.
- Products containing ammonia will remove the special layer that prevents the reflection of light. Rather use a soft, damp cloth or a feather duster. Paper towels will scratch the screen.
- Use ethyl alcohol if the screen is very dirty.

Laptops

The best place to put a laptop when working on it, is on a table or desk, not on your lap. A laptop will overheat on your lap and not only is this bad for the computer, it is especially unhealthy for men. Buy a special cushion for your laptop if you prefer to work on your lap.

Prevent muscle pain

To help prevent repetitive strain injury as a result of sitting in front of a computer for too long:

- Make sure your body is correctly aligned. The chair at your computer should offer sufficient support for your back and arms. Your feet should be on the floor and your bottom should be higher than your knees.

- Position the screen so that when seated you can touch it with an outstretched arm.
- The keyboard should be at elbow height and the mouse must be as close as possible to it.
- Get up and walk around regularly to stretch your legs and back.
- Listen to your body. If you have recurring or persistent neck or back problems, consult a doctor.

Clear your browsing history

Your browsing history keeps a record of every site you visit on the internet. This information can be used by others. Ensure it stays private by deleting the hard-drive information regularly.

Delete spyware

Adware and cookie files are often sent to a computer to spy on the user's search habits and preferences on the internet. People can use this information to obtain personal information, such as bank details and passwords. Protect your computer with good antivirus software that deletes cookies on a daily basis.

Delete files permanently

When you click "delete" on your computer, the file is not deleted permanently; it is simply moved to the recycle bin. And when you delete something from the recycle bin, although the record of the file is deleted, the content remains somewhere on your hard drive. Obtain a program that removes sensitive information permanently.

Golden rules of internet behaviour

- Treat other internet users as you would like to be treated yourself.
- Always be polite. Never become abusive or use bad language simply because you can hide behind an alias.
- Respect copyright. It is a criminal offence to use someone else's intellectual property without permission.
- Do not type in capital letters: it is as if you are shouting.
- Do not forward email messages that are clearly spam.

How to clean a camera

Open the parts of the camera that open and clean them using a bulb tool that blows air when squeezed, or compressed air. Use lens-cleaning fluid and a non-static cloth to polish the lens. Wipe the outside of the camera with a damp cloth and use a soft toothbrush to remove dust from hard-to-reach places. Clean dirty battery contacts with a soft pencil eraser.

Shoot better videos

- Use a tripod.
- Learn how to pan the camera, and to zoom in and out.
- Think about the composition of every shot.
- Buy a good-quality microphone and use it to do interviews.
- Try to structure your short film in such a way that it tells a story.

Notes

Notes

BLACK&DECKER
KR550CRE 550W
The Deckle Edge

HANDYMAN tips 10

Alternative solutions

"If you can't find a screwdriver, use a knife. If you break off the tip, it's an improved screwdriver."

Robert Fulghum

LADDERS

Stand firm

Placing the legs of a ladder in a pair of old tennis shoes will make it less likely to wobble.

That sinking feeling

If the legs of a ladder keep sinking into soft ground, place two tins of the same size under the legs.

Stash your tools

Drill some holes through the top rung of a wooden ladder to store your tools. Make sure the items fit snugly and will not fall through. Then you can carry the ladder around horizontally, tools and all.

Ladder safety

- Always maintain three-point contact with the ladder: two feet and one hand or two hands and one foot must always be on the ladder.
- If you need both hands to do the job, consider using a scaffold.
- The buckle on your belt or trousers must never be higher than the ladder rail.
- Only one person should be on the ladder at any one time.
- Do not carry building materials up a ladder. Rather hoist them up using ropes.

Secure wooden ladders

Make the rungs of a wooden ladder safer by painting them, sprinkling coarse sand over the wet paint and leaving to dry. The rungs will now offer a better grip.

DRILLS AND DRILLING

The right depth

- Slip a piece of plastic tubing onto the drill bit so that just the right depth you want to drill is sticking out.
- You can also stick masking tape around the bit at the required depth.

Keep a drill stand in place

Fix a piece of old tyre around the base of a drill stand to ensure that the objects being drilled do not move about.

Drilling glazed tiles

If you need to drill into a tile, mark the position with a cross of transparent adhesive tape. This will hold the drill bit in position long enough to be able to drill a hole.

Stop tiles cracking

Once you have drilled the hole in the tile and inserted a plug, it is important to make sure that the plug goes all the way through the tile before you insert the screw. This will prevent the tile from cracking.

Use an envelope

Stick an envelope to the wall below the spot where you plan to drill. The dust and cement will fall into the envelope. If you do not have an envelope handy, a piece of paper folded in half down the length and stuck to the wall will also do the trick.

Drill out old putty

Use an old countersinking bit on an electric drill to drill out putty from window frames.

Hole in water pipe

If you drill a hole in a water pipe by accident, turn off the water at the mains. Break out the plaster around the pipe with a chisel. Fill the hole with epoxy putty. Wait at least 24 hours before turning on the water again.

SUCCESSFUL SAWING

Candle wax for the blade

Rub candle wax onto the blade of a saw to help you cut wet wood accurately.

Placing the legs of a ladder in a pair of old tennis shoes will make it less likely to wobble.

If a screw needs to be inserted and you are unable to hold it, attach it to the end of the screw-driver with reusable putty.

Saw a small piece

If a very small piece of a plank needs to be sawn off, make it easier by clamping a second plank next to the one to be sawn. Position the end of the second plank about 2 cm past the end of the piece to be sawn off, then saw both planks at the same time.

Keep the angle small

The angle between the saw and the plank you are sawing should not be too big, otherwise it increases the chances of sawing skew. The ideal angle is 35 degrees.

Prevent wood cracking

Thin wooden planks have a tendency to crack and split when a nail is driven through them. Prevent this by drilling a small hole where you want to insert the nail. Then knock the nail through the hole.

Stop plywood splintering

Stick masking tape along the line where you plan to saw plywood, and it will not splinter.

Blow as you go

While sawing, it is a good idea to blow away the sawdust as you work so that the sawing line remains clearly visible.

Dirty blade

Clean a dirty saw blade with oven cleaner.

Jigsaw

- If you plan to cut a template out of a piece of wood using a jigsaw, apply a thick layer of a flour-and-water paste to the paper on which the template is drawn. Stick the wet template to the wood.
- Once it is dry, you will be able to cut out the template accurately. Then tear off the paper and lightly sand off any pieces that remain.

Sawdust filler

To fill a dent or a hole in wood, mix sawdust with a little wood glue and use it as a filler.

Offcuts

Cut offcuts of wood into different sizes and shapes, sand to a smooth finish and paint with colourful lead-free paint. The blocks make wonderful toys for small children.

Sandpaper for the sander

Instead of buying special sandpaper for your sander, you can use ordinary sandpaper cut neatly into three across the width. It is much cheaper.

DIY sander

Make your own mini sander by stuffing half a tennis ball with steel wool.

Magnetic screwdrivers

Magnetise your screwdriver to make it easier to hold the screws. It will also enable you to pick up dropped screws using the screwdriver. To do this, rub a magnet up and down the length of the screwdriver a few times.

Stick it there

If a screw needs to be inserted in a hard-to-reach spot and you are unable to hold it, attach it to the end of the screwdriver with reusable putty.

Get that screw loose

Loosen rusted nuts, bolts and screws by soaking them in lemon juice, cola, brake fluid or vinegar. Dip a tissue in the liquid and wrap it round the bolt or screw to be loosened.

Long-lasting bonds

Dip screws in glue before screwing them in and the bond will last much longer.

Hit the nail on the head

When hammering a nail, hold it a little way below the head and remember to keep your eye on the nail – not on the hammer!

Cardboard protection

If you have to put in a nail in an awkward spot, push it through a piece of cardboard first. Then you can hold the cardboard instead of the nail and keep your fingers out of the way. This also reduces the chance of damaging the surface with the hammer if you miss.

Soldering tips

- Screw two wooden clothes pegs on either side of a block of wood to hold the wire or rods that are to be soldered together. With the wires or rods held in place, you can concentrate on the soldering.
- Hold soldering work in place with pliers by tying an elastic band firmly around the handle. This will automatically keep the jaws closed. The heavier the pliers, the better they will keep the object in place.

Solder a water pipe

If you struggle to dry a water pipe completely so that it can be soldered, remove the crust from a slice of white bread, break the bread into pieces and stuff it into the pipe. The bread will absorb the moisture and you will be able to solder the pipe. Flush out the pipes well afterwards and the bread will dissolve in time.

Dirty soldering iron

Wipe a soldering iron on a damp sponge to clean it.

10.1 TOOLS

Hosepipe for better grip

Wrap pieces of hosepipe around the handles of tools and implements to give you a firmer grip.

Clamp glued objects

Use the clamp from a rotary mincer, or other piece of equipment that is screwed to a table, to clamp objects that need to be glued together.

Marking equipment

Mark equipment with wooden handles by writing your initials on the handle in nail polish. Light the nail polish and your initials will burn into the wood.

Old files

Sharpen an old file and use it as a chisel.

Protect chisels

Push short pieces of plastic tubing over the ends of chisels to protect them – and your fingers.

Sorting tip

Cut an opening in the side of an empty laundry softener bottle and use it to keep bolts, nails and screws as you sort them. Once the bottle is full, it is easy to pour the nails into another container through the mouth of the bottle.

Silica gel

Keep the silica gel that comes with packaging and put it in your tool box to keep tools shiny and tarnish-free.

10.2 WALLS

Clean bricks

Scrape white bricks clean using ammonia or a solution of a quarter of a cup of white vinegar in two litres of water.

Paint on bricks

Remove paint spatters from bricks by rubbing them off with another brick.

Crack in the wall

To disguise a crack in the wall, paint one coat of paint over the crack and then stick a piece of cotton fabric over the painted section. Paint over it again, and the crack will be less visible.

How to fill a hole or crack in the wall

- Press enough filler into the crack so that some is raised above the surface of the wall. When it is dry, sand the wall to a smooth finish.
- If there is a gap between the plaster and the skirting board, it should be filled using a filler that contains butyl, which can be pushed snugly into the gap.

Filler that holds

- Mix powdered crack filler with cold glue to create an excellent filler for cracks and holes in walls.
- Mix filler for walls with PVA paint to make an exceptionally hard filler that will shrink very little.

Neat filling

Mix crack filler in a sealable plastic bag. Cut a corner off the bag and you can squeeze out a line of filler directly into the crack or hole.

Home-made filler

Mix baby powder with paint in the colour you intend painting the wall, and use it to fill the cracks. It will not shrink.

TILING

The right tiles

If you are planning to tile a wall yourself, choose wall tiles and not floor tiles for the job. Floor tiles are often too heavy for tiling walls and can cause real problems.

Masking tape for sealing

Stick masking tape to the tiles and the bath when applying sealant between tiles and bath. Wait until the sealant is dry before removing the tape.

Applying grout

Use an old icing syringe to apply grout between tiles.

Mix batches of tiles

Before starting to lay wall tiles, it is a good idea to mix tiles from different batches to ensure an even distribution of colour.

Replacing a tile

If there is grout between the broken tiles, remove it first. Then use a chisel or something similar to hit the cracked tile hard in the middle. The tile should shatter and come away from the wall. When you remove the tile, you will see an imprint of the back of the tile on the dry glue. Apply glue to the new tile and place it exactly over the pattern.

WALLPAPER

Read the instructions

Read the information on the packaging. It should tell you, which type of glue should be used, whether it should be applied to the front or the back of the paper, and whether you can wash the wallpaper with soap and water afterwards.

Removing old wallpaper

The best way to remove wallpaper is to hire a steam machine from a hardware store and steam off the panels one by one. Start at the top and work your way down the wall. Stubborn areas can be treated with a sponge soaked in vinegar water. Unfortunately, wallpaper on plasterboard has to be removed dry.

Prepare wall for papering

Scrub off all the glue residue with a hard brush and hot water. Fill any holes and make sure the entire surface of the wall is smooth. The day before you intend hanging the wallpaper, spread a layer of wallpaper glue over all the treated areas. Doing this will help the wallpaper stick better.

Before starting to lay wall tiles, it is a good idea to mix tiles from different batches to ensure an even distribution of colour.

Chimney as focal point

If the chimney is the focal point of the room you want to wallpaper, it is best to start there. Hang the first panel in the middle of the chimney or, depending on the width of the paper, make the join run right down the middle. Make the panels run round the front corners, then move on to the rest of the wall. The sides of the chimney should be papered last. If the pattern does not match perfectly, it will not be noticeable.

Wallpaper shrinkage

As wallpaper dries, it should shrink evenly. However, sometimes a join may be exposed in the process. You can fix this by applying a strip of latex wall paint in the same colour as the wallpaper over the gap.

Troublesome air bubbles

Stubborn air bubbles that remain under wallpaper even when dry can be treated with an injection. Buy a syringe with a thickish needle from a pharmacy. Thin the wallpaper adhesive a little and inject it into the bubble, then use a roller to flatten the bubble.

Cut slightly longer

When cutting wallpaper, always add an extra 10–15 cm. This will give you the chance to match the patterns exactly. Cut off the edge by pressing the paper firmly against the wall with a palette knife and trimming it with a craft knife.

Wet cloth

Use a wet cloth or sponge to wipe glue residue from the paper when you have finished hanging it. This also helps the wallpaper dry neatly.

Bored with wallpaper?

If you grow tired of wallpaper and it is still firmly attached to the wall, you can paint over it. Apply a good undercoat before the topcoat.

Wall stickers

When sticking a large wall sticker to the wall, ensure that the surface is completely free of grease by washing the wall with ammonia. If the edges keep coming loose, stick the corners in place with glue for plastic, or double-sided tape.

10.3 PAINT

Removing old paint

Chemical paint strippers remain one of the most effective means of removing paint from wood and other surfaces. Wear thick rubber gloves, eye protection and preferably an effective mask to prevent the toxic fumes from being inhaled. If you are using a blow torch to remove paint, keep a hosepipe or bucket of water to hand in case the wood catches alight.

Home-made paint stripper

1. Dissolve 250 ml washing soda in 500 ml boiling water. Add 500 ml quicklime. The mixture should form a thin paste. Warning: quicklime reacts vigorously when mixed with water and can cause injury.
2. Apply two thin coats of the cold mixture to the surface to be stripped.
3. Leave for 24 hours and then scrub off and hose down with water.
4. Neutralise the surface with equal parts vinegar and water.

Screw out wall plugs

Plastic wall plugs used to insert screws or nails can be screwed out using a corkscrew.

Petroleum-jelly protection

Before you start painting, apply petroleum jelly or glycerine to windows, door knobs and light fittings. This way, paint spatters will be easy to wipe off.

Dry brushes in a flash

Place in a plastic bag a paintbrush that has been soaking in turpentine. Close the bag securely and strike the brush to dry it. This gets the brushers dry quickly, and also avoids messy cloths and newspaper, and paint spatters everywhere.

Old paintbrush

You can extend the life of an old paintbrush with curled-up bristles by giving it a trim. Hold a razor blade against a comb and draw the comb through the bristles.

To determine which kind of paint has been used on a wall, place a piece of cotton wool dipped in ethyl alcohol on the paint.

Paraffin for brushes

Cleaning paintbrushes with paraffin instead of turpentine keeps the bristles soft.

Easy cleaning

Wrap the metal section of the paintbrush in masking tape before you start painting and it will be a lot easier to clean afterwards.

Clamp brushes together

Use large plastic or metal bulldog clips to keep the bristles of paintbrushes together. Hang the clips from a nail in the wall and this also becomes a useful way to store your brushes.

Hardened brushes

- Soften a paintbrush that has become hardened with paint by soaking it in Jeyes Fluid and then washing it with green household soap.
- You can also boil the brush in vinegar and then wash it in hot soapy water.

String on a tin

Tie a piece of thick string over the top of the paint tin and use it to wipe excess paint off the paintbrush.

Insulation tape

Use insulation tape instead of masking tape to tape off areas when painting. Insulation tape is easier to remove afterwards and can then be used on the next section.

Narrow before wide

When painting frames and doors, always paint the narrow sections before the broad ones. And paint horizontal parts before vertical ones.

Clean paint

Blow dust off the top of the paint tin before opening it otherwise the dust may end up in the paint. If the paint has already got dirty, transfer it to another tin through a nylon stocking that has been folded double.

Acrylic paint thinners

Use acrylic paint thinners to thin water-based paint. The thinners extend the drying time of the paint, giving you longer to apply it neatly. Thinners also help the paint grip better.

Paint no-go areas

You cannot paint over oil, polish or wax.

Which kind of paint?

To determine which kind of paint has been used on a wall, place a piece of cotton wool dipped in ethyl alcohol on the paint. If the paint becomes tacky and soft, it is acrylic paint. If not, it is water-based.

Tester-sized bottles of paint

Pour a little paint of every colour used in your house into small glass bottles with a tight-fitting lid. Keep the containers where they are easily accessible. Then, when you want to do a touch-up, there is no need to dig out the big tin from the garage or storeroom.

Prevent drips

When painting a ceiling using a block brush, the paint often dribbles down the handle of the brush. To prevent this, push the handle through a thick sponge that will collect excess paint.

Protect your hair

Wear a shower cap when painting ceilings and walls.

Avoid wool

The fibres in wool attract paint, so avoid wearing woollen clothes when painting.

Clean paint tins

- Fold a strip of tinfoil around the rim of the paint tin. This will keep the rim clean and you will be able to close the lid properly afterwards.
- Store paint tins upside down to prevent a skin forming on the top of the paint.

Paint spatters

When you paint large surfaces quickly, the paint tends to spatter. To help prevent this, leave the paint rollers in hot water with a capful of turpentine for an hour before you start painting.

Paper plate

Stick a paper plate under paint and varnish tins before opening them. This will stop the contents spilling on the floor.

Glow-in-the-dark light switches

Paint light switches in the passage and outside the bathroom in luminous paint so that you can find them easily in the dark.

Drying spray paint

Place an item that has been spray-painted on a piece of wire netting to dry and avoid the hassle of it sticking to the table or newspaper.

Reuse plastic bags

Use old plastic bags as gloves when painting.

Old toothbrushes

An old toothbrush is very useful for painting hard-to-reach corners.

Paint with a broom

Save time by painting the ceiling using a broom.

Paint with sponge

Paint with strips of foam rubber used for packaging. This not only saves on a paintbrush, but also gets the job done faster and ensures even coverage.

Painting doors

If you intend painting a door using a brush, remove any loose bristles first by running the brush over sandpaper a few times.

Painting steps

When painting a flight of stairs, paint every second step so that the stairs can be used while the paint is drying. Once the paint is dry, you can paint the remaining steps.

Painting wooden chairs

Knock a nail halfway into the bottom of each leg of the chair. Place the chair on newspaper and you can paint without the legs sticking to the paper or the floor.

10.4 DOORS

Hanging a door

Apply a coat of transparent varnish to a door that still has to be painted, before hanging it. By doing this, you will be able to see all the fingerprints and grease marks that are likely to get onto the door during the process of hanging it. Carefully remove all marks before applying the next coat of paint.

Turning a door

To turn a door that opens inwards so that it opens outwards, you will need to turn the entire door frame around.

Split the difference

If you need to take off more than 5 mm from a door to make it fit, divide the difference between the top and bottom or left-hand and right-hand sides of the door. The instructions that come with the door usually state the maximum number of millimetres that can be removed.

Candle wax for screws

Screws are easier to turn in the hinges of a door if you rub them with candle wax first.

Horizontal holes

To ensure that a door is hung properly, it is very important that the holes are perfectly horizontal. Use a drill stand when drilling the holes.

Use masking tape

- Before you start drilling holes in a door, it is a good idea to mark the top left-hand corner of the front of the door with masking tape. This will save you a lot of hassle later.
- When you remove a door, store the hinge pins in the hinges so they do not get lost.

Before you start drilling holes in a door, mark the top left-hand corner of the front of the door with masking tape. This will save you a lot of hassle later.

Creaky hinges

Apply petroleum jelly or dishwashing liquid to creaky hinges. You can also fix a rattling door by injecting a few balls of transparent silicone sealant into the corners of the frame.

Sticking door

Place a piece of sandpaper under the door and open and close it a number of times. The part that is sticking should be sanded off.

Lock that sticks

Push graphite shavings from a pencil into a lock that is difficult to open.

Key broken in the lock

Using pliers with a very sharp nose, carefully try to remove the piece of key from the lock. If this does not work, cut a narrow piece from a saw blade, teeth and all. Insert the strip into the keyhole with the teeth facing outwards and try to hook the key in this way. Failing this, unscrew the entire lock and try to jiggle the key loose with a piece of wire.

10.5 GENERAL

Rigid water pipes

Soften a plastic pipe so that it can slide over another pipe by leaving it in boiling water for a while.

Noisy water pipes

- Water pipes can make a noise for a number of reasons. Ensure that the water pressure is correct, check the valves and also make sure that the pipe is firmly attached to the wall.
- Sometimes the solution lies in closing the hot-water mains, opening all the taps in the house and then closing the mains again. This will get rid of air in the pipes.

Gutters

- Check your gutters to make sure there are no screws or other metal objects lying in the gutters that will cause the pipes to rust.
- Gutters are easy to clean using a plastic dough scraper or spatula from the kitchen. If debris in the gutter has become compacted and difficult to remove, wet it a bit using a hosepipe and dig it out with a small garden spade.

Roof tiles

If you need to replace a tile on the roof, it is the ideal opportunity to check the rafters and surrounding tiles for wear and tear.

Sliding doors that stick

Rub candle wax or clear polish on the runners of a sliding door to make it easier to slide open and shut.

10.6 ELECTRICITY

Electric wiring
Use nail clippers to strip insulation material from electric wiring.

Solder wires with ease
It is simple to hold electric wires in place with a home-made clamp: insert a long nail through the springs of two clothes pegs and attach the large grooves of the pegs to a screwdriver. Then you can use the small grooves on the pegs for the wires.

Safe extension cords
Never lay a temporary extension cord under a carpet where it can easily cause an accident. Always place such cords where there is the least amount of foot traffic.

How to store electrical cords
Drill two holes in a rectangular plank and knock two long wooden dowels into them. Wrap electrical cords around the dowels in a figure of eight.

Adaptor plugs
Always use an adaptor plug if the wall plug does not have the same number of pins as there are holes in the wall socket.

Safe fuses
To help prevent fires, make sure you buy a fuse of the right size when one needs replacing.

Hot adaptors are dangerous
Wall plugs and adaptors must always remain cool to the touch. If a plug or adaptor gets hot, replace or repair it immediately.

How to thread wires
If you need to thread an electric wire through a thin tube, a vacuum cleaner can come in handy. Attach the vacuum hose to the tube securely using masking

tape. Attach a small piece of paper to some thin cord and suck the paper through the pipe using the vacuum cleaner. Then tie the other side of the cord to the cable and pull it through the tube.

Safe distribution board

When installing an electrical distribution board, make sure that there are no crossed wires. Wires that touch can overheat and short-circuit. If you are in any doubt, consult an electrician.

Wall plugs and adaptors must always remain cool to the touch. If a plug or adaptor gets hot, replace or repair it immediately.

Notes

Notes

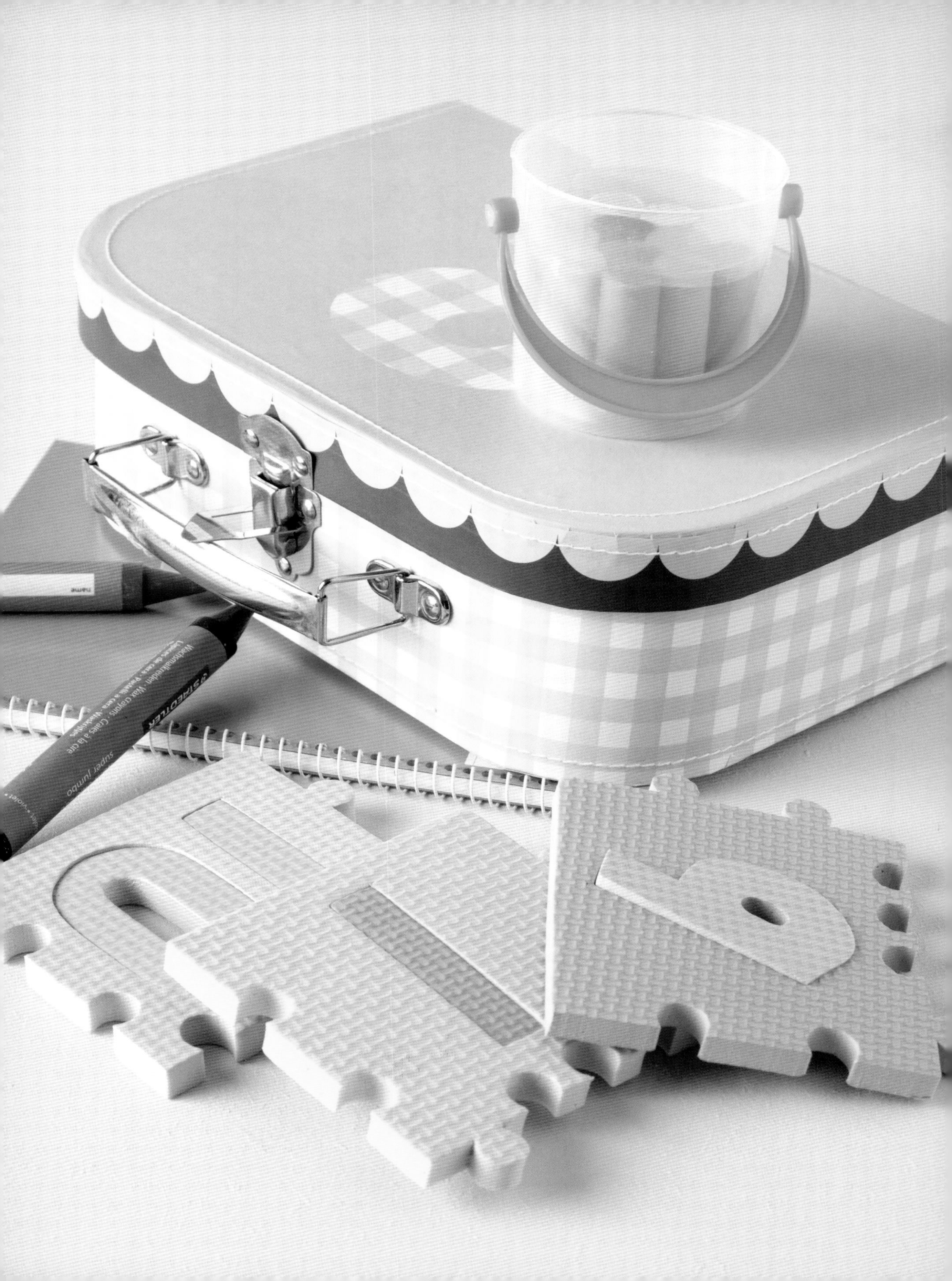

the FAMILY

11

Love is what matters

"Love begins by taking care of the closest ones – the ones at home."

Mother Teresa

11.1 BABIES

Place a hot-water bottle in baby's cot when you take her out for feeding at night.

Disposable nappies and the environment

Until recently, it used to take one disposable nappy 90 years to decompose. However, nappies manufactured these days are far cleaner environmentally. When choosing between cloth nappies and disposables, consider that disposables place a burden on the environment during manufacture and as waste, while cloth nappies place a burden on the environment every time they are washed. On the other hand, the same cloth nappies can be used for more than one child and children who wear them are generally toilet-trained earlier.

Bottles

A baby will have less trouble holding a smooth plastic bottle if you cover it with a coloured sock.

Funnel

To make it easier to dispense formula into a baby's bottle, cut a funnel from the top of a plastic cooldrink bottle.

Hole in the teat

You can enlarge the hole in a teat using a hot needle. Remove the black mark that is left behind using a little butter and a dry cloth. Wash the teat well before using it again.

Sterilise baby's bottles

Pour a small amount of water into the bottle, pop in the teat and heat on high in the microwave for a few seconds. When the water boils, the bottle has been sterilised. Leave bottles to cool before removing them.

Stained drinking cups

A drinking cup that has become stained by fruit juice can be cleaned using hot water and a little bicarbonate of soda.

Sour-smelling bottles

A teaspoon of uncooked rice and hot water placed in a dirty baby's bottle will absorb all the acidity of sour milk and leave the bottle sparkling clean.

Bath time

Apply a little petroleum jelly to baby's forehead so that the shampoo does not run into his eyes.

Warm bed

Place a hot-water bottle in baby's cot when you take her out for feeding at night and the bed will stay lovely and warm.

Multipurpose trolley

Cover a small vegetable trolley in attractive paper, plastic or fabric and use it to store baby's essentials. You can move it around the house and everything you need will be on hand.

Washing baby clothes

- To help prevent allergies and skin reactions, it is best to wash a newborn baby's clothes separately at first in a detergent developed specially for sensitive skins. Such products usually contain no colourants or perfume.
- Toss all knitted booties and other small items of clothing into a pillowcase, lingerie bag or old stocking and tie a knot in the top before putting the whole lot in the washing machine.

Inflatable seat

Inflate the tube from an old tyre and let baby sit in it to prevent him getting hurt when falling over.

Make your own wipes

- *With oil:* Buy a roll of strong, two-ply toilet paper and saturate it with baby oil. Remove the cardboard inner roll and pull out the first "wipe" starting from the inside. Keep the paper in a plastic container with a lid.
- *With soap:* Combine four cups boiling water, four tablespoons baby soap and three tablespoons baby cream. Pour into two plastic containers for wipes. Cut the sheets of a roll of paper towel in half and pack them into the liquid. Put the lids on the containers and turn them over so that the fluid can permeate the paper.

Protect baby's legs

When baby starts crawling, you can protect her legs and clothes by pulling an old pair of men's socks over her legs.

Smooth shoes

Stick plasters on the soles of baby's new shoes to give them a better grip.

Mirror magic

Babies love looking at their reflection in the mirror. Keep a small hand mirror in your handbag to help keep baby entertained when you have to wait somewhere.

Finger puppets

Make fun finger puppets from scraps of material to amuse baby.

Keep doors closed

When baby starts to crawl, it is a good idea to buy childproof locks for cupboard doors. You can also use wide elastic bands to keep doorknobs together. Glass doors can be kept shut using reusable putty.

Safe wall sockets

Cover all electrical sockets in the house with plastic wall-socket covers.

Useful storage

Hang a plastic shelving unit (often used for shoes) where you bath baby and store all the bath supplies in one easy-to-reach place.

Make a noisy book for baby

1. Cut out coloured printed cotton in pieces as large as the double pages of an average baby book. Cut out enough pieces so that each page has a back as well.
2. Sew the sides of the pages together and stuff with cotton stuffing and pieces of foil wrapping paper so that it makes a noise when baby handles the book. Sew the stuffed pages together.
3. Place all the double pages on top of each other and stitch down the spine of the book. You can also sew material with different textures on the pages.
4. For older children, work buttons, zips, bells, and even a part of a shoe for threading laces babygros onto the book.

Babygros

Use men's T-shirts with interesting designs on them to make ultra-cute babygros for cool tots.

Fridge magnets for kids

Use fabric to make oversized fridge magnets for toddlers. Cut out the pattern twice and stitch a magnetic strip between the two layers of fabric.

How to take better photos of babies

- Avoid dressing baby in too many clothes, which will swamp him. Choose simple accessories and carefully consider the choice of colour.
- Make sure that the background or blanket does not reflect too much light.
- Take lots of close-ups and try to eliminate as much background and unnecessary detail as possible. Also take close-ups of baby's feet and hands.
- Ensure that you and the camera are level with baby if you want lovely shots with good eye contact.

Five golden rules

- If your child wants to show you something, stop what you are doing and give her the attention required. It is important to spend short periods in each other's company often and to do fun things together.
- Touch your child frequently. Most children like being hugged and holding your hand.
- Talk to your children about things that interest them and tell them about your day.
- Praise your children when they have done something well.
- Bored children are sure to get under their parents' feet. Make sure you have something on hand to keep them busy.

When baby won't stop crying

- Take baby for a walk if the weather allows. The change of environment could help baby settle, and the fresh air will do you both good.
- Go for a drive. Most babies fall asleep in the car.
- Dance with your baby. Turn the music up, hold baby securely and move to the rhythm.
- Give baby a warm bath.
- Ask older children to play hide and seek with you and the baby.

11.2 TODDLERS AND YOUNG CHILDREN

Meal ideas

- Make a sausage dog using different sized sausages.
- Make a caterpillar using a filled flatbread, such as a tortilla or roti, that you cut into rounds, using tomato for the head and pretzel sticks for the legs.
- Build a face on a pizza.
- Freeze pieces of canned fruit in home-made ice lollies.
- Build a house using different kinds of bread and toppings.

Food too hot?

Cool hot baby food quickly by placing an ice cube in it.

A variety of foods

Expose your children to a variety of tastes, textures and flavours from a young age. This will encourage them to try new dishes and limit fussiness.

Ice-cream cones

Serve children their dessert in ice-cream cones so that it is easier for them to eat.

Best toy ever

One of the best toys for a toddler is a big empty cardboard box. Also give him some crayons to decorate the box to his heart's content.

Low mirror

Mount a low mirror in the bathroom so that the children can see themselves.

Cover up

The ideal apron for a toddler is an old shirt of dad's buttoned up the back.

Clothing sizes

Age	Height	Weight	Size	
3–4	99–107 cm	15–17 kg	4	XS
4–5	107–114 cm	17–20 kg	5	S
5–6	114–122 cm	20–23 kg	6	S
6–7	122–130 cm	23–26 kg	6/7	M
7–8	130–137 cm	26–30 kg	8	M
8–9	137–145 cm	30–34 kg	10	L
9–10	145–152 cm	34–39 kg	12	L
10+	152–157 cm	39–45 kg	14	XL

Smooth swing

Stick a small rubber mat or bath stickers onto a swing seat to give it extra grip.

Holiday activity case

Pack a bag or old cardboard school suitcase with interesting activities for the holiday, and give it to your toddler only once you get in the car. Include, for example, a jigsaw puzzle, colouring-in book and crayons, a bag of blocks, storybooks, a packet of sweets and a board game.

Beach toys

Take the buckets, spades and other beach toys to the beach in a washing basket and it will be easy to rinse everything clean together afterwards.

Tractor tyre

Use an old tractor tyre to make a sand pit for young children.

Bigger bubbles

Add a few drops of glycerine to the soapy water children use to blow bubbles. This will help them blow bigger, longer-lasting bubbles.

Messy hair

If a doll's hair has become tangled and messy, leave it in fabric softener for a few hours. Rinse and comb smooth.

Roll-on paints

Use empty roll-on deodorant bottles to make roll-on paints that will provide toddlers withhours of fun. Remove the ball, pour in the paint and replace the ball.

Find an old handbag and fill it with old perfume bottles, imitation jewellery and make-up.

MAKE YOUR OWN PLAY DOUGH

Recipe 1

Mix 500 ml flour, 250 ml salt and 15 ml cooking oil into a stiff dough. Knead the dough until it is elastic.

Recipe 2

For extra elasticity, add two teaspoons cream of tartar and stir the mixture over a low heat.

Recipe 3

- Combine 750 ml flour, 250 ml salt, one tablespoon alum, three tablespoons cooking oil and 500 ml boiling water.
- Use food colouring to colour the dough. You can also add glitter for extra sparkle.

Papier mâché

Buy a packet of wallpaper glue and use it to make beautiful papier mâché models. Make up only a small amount of glue at a time because it keeps quite a long time. Create the form using wire netting or inflated balloons, and cover with small strips of newspaper that you have soaked in wallpaper glue. Wait until one layer is dry before covering it with a second one. Once the model is completely dry, paint it.

Granny's handbag

Find an old handbag and fill it with old perfume bottles, imitation jewellery and make-up. The grandchildren will have great fun playing with it when next they come to visit.

Never give a toddler more than two options. Too much choice confuses children and makes them insecure.

Dressing-up trunk

Children love dressing up. Keep clothes and other items suitable for dressing up in a trunk or large suitcase, and be on the lookout for unusual hats, shoes and other accessories at markets and bazaars.

Play mat

Cut a circle out of thick, washable fabric and attach large curtain rings around the edge. Thread a cord through the rings. Then, when your child has finished playing, pull the cord to form a sack with all the toys in it and hang it up for next time.

Talk so they listen

- Before giving children an instruction, you need to know exactly what you expect of them. Also decide beforehand whether you are giving the child the option to say no, or if you expect her to do what you say.
- Go to the child, make sure you have her attention, and explain calmly what you want done.
- Think about what you are going to do if the child does not respond as you would like.
- Make sure that any punishment is logical and in proportion to the importance of the task.

Difficult choices

Never give a toddler more than two options. Too much choice confuses children and makes them insecure.

Sore ears when flying

Many children are troubled by sore ears during ascent and descent when flying. Give older children chewing gum; chewing helps reduce the pressure in their ears. Sucking a dummy or drinking a small amount of milk from a bottle should help reduce the pressure in babies' ears.

All read out

If you need to keep small children occupied quietly and they are not interested in listening to a story, you could always give them a catalogue to look at. Give them each a pen and get them to mark what they would like to "buy".

Child's play

- Make a hole in the edge of an empty margarine tub and thread a cord through it. Now it looks like a car or truck into which you can load things and will offer a child hours of amusement.
- Thread a number of empty cotton reels onto a piece of garter elastic and attach it somewhere interesting for a toddler to play with.
- Cut drinking straws into rounds and encourage young children to thread them onto wool to make "jewellery".

Make-it-better bear

- Sew a bear out of towelling and stuff it with sawdust or dried lentils.
- The bear can be heated in the microwave to soothe a sore tummy or frozen in the freezer to put on bumps and bruises. Add a few drops of essential oil, such as lavender, to the lentils to help calm an unsettled baby.

Rotate toys

Pack away half of your child's toys at the top of the cupboard, and rotate the toys after a few weeks. Your child will be thrilled with his "new" toys.

Hospital visits

- If possible, arrange for your child to have a tour of the hospital before admission. Ask whether a sympathetic nurse could walk around with you and explain everything to your child.
- Encourage the child to take a favourite soft toy or blanket along.
- Explain to the child exactly what is going to happen and assure him that he can expect lots of spoiling when he gets home. It helps the child to have something positive to look forward to.

Pack away half of your child's toys at the top of the cup-board, and rotate the toys after a few weeks.

- Organise your schedule so that you can spend as much time as possible with your child at the hospital.
- Keep yourself informed about the child's medication and treatment plan.

Hospitals can get very cold, so make sure your child is warm enough.

Listening pleasure

When heading on a long car journey, get hold of an audio book that the whole family can listen to. This works better than trying to accommodate everyone's tastes in music and encourages a feeling of togetherness. And it is far better than a car filled with isolated children with headphones on.

Notes

your PETS

12

Considering getting a pet? Ask yourself:

Why do I want a pet?
Do I have enough time to give a pet the attention it needs?
Do I have enough time and money to care for a pet?
Does the animal suit my personality and situation?
Who will look after my pet when I go away on holiday?

12.1 AQUARIUM

Develop an ecosystem

It takes a long time to create the ideal, balanced ecosystem in an aquarium. Patience is the only solution.

Every day

- In order to maintain a clean aquarium at all times, it is important to measure the temperature of the water every day.
- If it gets too warm, algae will multiply twice as fast.
- Adding a little salt to a freshwater aquarium will help keep algae in check. Ask your pet shop for guidelines on the right amount to use.
- Check for sick or dead fish every day, and remove them from the tank immediately.
- Make sure that the pump and filter are working at full strength.
- Wash your hands thoroughly before putting them into the fish tank. Creams and ointments that may be on your skin could make your fish very ill and even kill them.

Rain water

It is better for tropical fish to have the aquarium filled with rain water than tap water.

Goldfish

- A goldfish in a bowl should never be allowed to stand in the sun.
- One goldfish needs at least two litres of water to be comfortable.

Lime in the water

Too much lime in the water? Place a piece of granite, basalt or slate in the bottom of the aquarium to prevent lime deposits.

Snails

Freshwater snails help keep an aquarium clean. If there are too many of them, put a lettuce leaf into the aquarium. The snails will be attracted to it and a few hours later you will be able to remove the leaf and the snails.

Happy fish

Fish flourish when the temperature of the water is just right, feeding has been adjusted to their needs and the water is crystal clear. Cloudy water means that the aquarium is dirty and must be cleaned.

Clean glass

- Clean the outside of the aquarium glass with salt and vinegar.
- Brush the inside of the aquarium with a dog toothbrush.

Disinfect gravel

Every now and then, clean the gravel in the bottom of the fish tank thoroughly by boiling it for 10 minutes.

Fish food

Give baby fish a block of yeast to nibble on.

Outdoor fish pond

If you live in an area that gets very cold in winter, remember that a fish pond will not freeze over if a ball is left floating in it.

12.2 HAMSTERS

A good night's sleep

Golden hamsters are lovely pets but are especially active at night. Do not keep a hamster in the bedroom if you want to get a good night's sleep.

Loneliness

Hamsters are content to be alone. Be aware that if you put two males together, they will fight.

Cleanliness

Hamsters are cleaner than mice. They always leave their droppings in the same spot and it is therefore easier to clean their cage.

Nutrition

Buy specialised hamster feed for your pet and spoil him with a piece of apple or carrot every now and then.

Cool as a cucumber

- During very hot weather, help your hamster stay cool by replacing his drinking water with water from the fridge.
- You could also pop a block of ice in the cage.
- Ensure that there is enough clean drinking water at all times.
- Place the cage in a cool spot in the house.
- Feed your hamster pieces of cucumber.

Extreme cold

Make sure the hamster has enough material to build a warm nest. Hamsters that get too cold will go into hibernation and probably not survive it. Ensure that the cage is not in a draught.

12.3 DOGS

Consistency is very important when training a dog. Make sure that all members of the family apply the same rules.

Behaviour

- From a very young age, teach your children to stay away from unfamiliar dogs. It is better to wait for the dog to approach them than to approach a dog they do not know.
- Always allow a dog to smell your hand before you touch his head or try to rub his back.
- Dogs that do not know you should never be approached from above, as dogs regard this as a threat.
- Find out about the dog's nature from the owner before allowing a young child to approach it.

Cost

- Dogs are not cheap pets. Before getting a dog, make sure you are in a position to pay the vet's bills if the dog gets sick as well as the cost of the inoculations your dog will need.
- Dog food is also expensive, especially if the dog is large. If you are not absolutely sure you are able to care for a dog financially, rather don't get one.

Choosing a puppy

- Check whether the puppy is lively, as a lethargic one may be ill.
- Are its eyes clear with no signs of infection of the tear glands?
- Is its nose cold?
- Are its ears clean inside and do they smell healthy?
- Are its gums pink and firm?
- Is its coat shiny and clean?
- Does it have dandruff in its coat?
- Make sure that the puppy has been dewormed and does not have fleas.

Buying a pedigree dog

- If you are interested in a pure breed, it is best to buy from a breeder who is accredited by KUSA (the Kennel Union of South Africa), the body that controls the registration of pedigree dogs in South Africa, and that can provide a KUSA registration certificate for the puppy.

- Also make sure you receive a vet's certificate regarding the puppy's health and inoculation status.

Training

Never give a puppy an old shoe to play with and chew. Dogs cannot distinguish between old shoes and new ones! Also think twice about giving a puppy a soft toy if there are small children in the house, as the puppy may steal their soft toys instead.

Inoculations

Inoculation	Puppies, younger than 16 weeks	Adult dogs, older than 16 weeks	Booster	Importance
Canine parvo-virus, adenovirus and distemper	First dose at 6–8 weeks and then every 3–4 weeks until 12–14 weeks	Two doses 3–4 weeks apart	Every 3 years unless the vet advises otherwise	Compulsory inoculation
Rabies	First dose at 3 months, to be repeated once after 9 months	Two doses a month apart	Every 3 years	Compulsory inoculation
Parainfluenza virus	First dose at 6–8 weeks, repeated 3–4 weeks later up to and including 12–14 weeks	Single dose	Every 3 years	Not compulsory. Used by breeders and kennels.
Bordetella bronchiseptica	Discuss with vet	Not applicable	Not applicable	Not compulsory. Used by breeders and kennels.
Leptospira	First dose at 12 weeks, repeated at 14–16 weeks	Two doses 2–4 weeks apart	Annual	Only on advice of a vet

Herpes virus	Not applicable	Bitch is inoculated when on heat or 2 weeks before puppies are born	Not applicable	Not compulsory. Used by breeders and kennels where herpes virus has been identified.
Coronavirus	Usually combined with the parvo, adeno and distemper inoculation	Two doses 3–4 weeks apart	Annual	Not compulsory. Used when dogs are often exposed to large numbers of other dogs.

Tick-tock comfort

If your puppy cries in the night, place an alarm clock on the floor near his bed. The ticking of the clock should comfort him.

One set of rules

Consistency is very important when training a dog. Make sure that all members of the family apply the same rules.

Deterrents

- Sprinkle pepper where you do not want the puppy doing his business. You can also use baby powder.
- Sprinkle baby powder on the grass when camping to keep dogs away – the powder makes them sneeze.

Food bowl

Buy your dog a hard food bowl, without crevices where bacteria can multiply. If the bowl keeps sliding around, stick a rubber ring on the bottom.

Milk and water

Always put a bowl of water down even if your dog prefers milk.

If your dog becomes hot

Gradually wet the dog with cool water, but do not hose him down or he could go into shock. Rather place wet towels over his body and keep him cool with water. Do not try to pour water down the dog's throat; make sure he is able to breathe properly. Try to take his temperature – if it is below 39 °C, the dog has recovered. Dry the dog well and offer him some water. Get him checked out by a vet to make sure there are no lasting ill effects.

Travelling with dogs

If you are taking your dog on a long car trip, give him only a third of the usual amount of food beforehand. Rather feed him small amounts when you stop along the way.

Bath time

- Dogs tend to get cold very easily, so try not to bath your dog too often.
- If you bath a dog in a large amount of water, put cotton wool in his ears to keep the water out.

Remove matted hair

Use a needlework unpicker to cut matted hair from your dog's coat.

Chewing gum in dog's coat

Rub chewing gum out of your dog's coat with a little peanut butter.

Stairs

Teach a puppy to climb stairs from a fairly young age, but do not overdo it. Get him to practise climbing 10 stairs once a week and gradually increase the number as he gets older. Climbing too many stairs could affect his muscle development.

Prevent worms

- Mix raw grated carrot into your dog's food regularly to help prevent worms.
- A piece of aloe crystal, half the size of the nail on your little finger, added to the dog's drinking water will also control parasites.

On a chain

- If you have no alternative but to chain your dog up on your property, make sure that the chain is long enough to give the dog plenty of room to roam about. Ensure that there is no way the dog can become entangled in the chain.
- Make sure there is enough shade as well as adequate shelter in the event of bad weather, as well as plenty of drinking water within easy reach.

Licking wounds

Rub aloe juice around a wound to stop the dog licking it. Tea tree oil is an antiseptic and will also prevent licking.

Collar

Remember to adjust the collar of growing animals regularly.

Not too fat

Stuffing your dog with unhealthy treats is very bad for his health and can be regarded as a form of cruelty to animals.

No chewing

Rub bandages or plasters a dog has to wear after an injury with soap to stop him chewing on them.

Keeps fleas away

- Stuff a few handfuls of cedar balls or shavings into your dog's mattress to keep fleas away and neutralise nasty smells.
- You could also place wild wormwood, tansy, khaki bush, rosemary and lavender in cushions and mattresses to deter pests.

Warm bed

Keep your dog's kennel warm in winter by placing a sheet of polystyrene under the floor covering.

12.4 CATS

Weaning kittens

- Small kittens can start on solid food from the age of about four weeks, but then they still need milk from their mother.
- The right time to take a kitten away from its mother is seven weeks of age.

Kitty toilet

Teach a young kitten where to do his business by throwing his stools in the tray of cat litter. The kitten will follow his nose and is likely to head straight for the litter tray next time.

Litter tray

Place a newspaper in the bottom of the tray before filling it with litter to make the tray easier to clean.

Scratching post

Teach a kitten where to sharpen his nails from a young age. If you do not want to buy a scratching post, make one by sticking a scrap of carpeting to a plank or against a wall.

Tinfoil deterrent

- Stick tinfoil on the backs of chairs and in other places you want to keep cat and dog free. Animals hate it!
- You could also dab a little vinegar on places where you do not want the cats to linger.

Inoculations

Kittens should be inoculated against various feline diseases for the first time between six and nine weeks. Two to four weeks later, a second dose will be administered, and after that the cat should receive a booster every year or at least every two years.

Sick cat

A sick cat usually has dry eyes, a dull, fluffed up coat and a dry nose.

Sterilisation

- It is an old wives' tale that a cat should have kittens before being sterilised. A female cat should be sterilised at between six and nine months.
- Male cats that are neutered will stop marking their territory. This should also be done from the age of about six months.

Hair loss

If you have an older cat that is losing its hair, add approximately two teaspoons of active yeast to its milk. Repeat for three days.

Hairballs

It is normal for cats to bring up hairballs. However, if your cat struggles to get rid of them and gags continuously, he needs help. Brush long-haired cats to remove loose hairs from their coats. Also add some butter to the cat's food and make sure there is enough fibre in his diet. Vegetables are a good source of fibre.

Whiskers

Do not cut off a cat's whiskers. He uses them to find his way in the dark, among other things.

Clean eyes

Clean cats' eyes gently using cotton wool dipped in warm water. Start in the outer corner and wipe in the direction of the nose.

No dog food

Dog food is bad for cats and they should not be given it to eat.

Onions

Onions are poisonous to cats and dogs. Sulfoxides and disulphides, which occur naturally in onions and garlic, cannot be digested by cats and dogs, and may lead to anaemia over time. However, the concentrations of these substances in garlic are not high enough to make a cat sick.

Freedom from fleas

- Make your cat's bed a flea-free zone by stuffing his cushion with one of the following: lavender, coriander seeds, sage, chamomile flowers or rosemary.
- Add yeast to your cat's food to help deter fleas. You can give dogs yeast and garlic, but too much garlic is not good for a cat.
- Spray your cat and his bedding with undiluted aloe juice.

If you have an older cat that is losing its hair, add approximately two teaspoons of active yeast to its milk. Repeat for three days.

Coffee grounds

Throw coffee grounds into pot plants to deter cats.

Keep pets away from electrical cords

Paint old-fashioned bitter aloe, which used to be used on children's nails to stop them biting them, on electrical cords your pets may chew.

12.5 RABBITS

Long teeth

Give rabbits hard, dry bread to chew on to keep their teeth short.

Linseed

Add linseed to the rabbit feed to keep your pet's coat shiny.

Long nails

Special nail clippers are available for cutting rabbits' nails. Take care not to cut the nails too short. With white nails it is easy to see where the nail bed starts because the nail becomes darker there. However, with black nails you will have to be extra careful.

Rabbits and guinea pigs

Do not keep rabbits and guinea pigs in the same hutch – they are just too different and cannot communicate with each other. What is more, a rabbit could easily injure a guinea pig, either accidentally or intentionally.

12.6 BIRDS

The right cage
Birds that live in a cage permanently need at least three times their wingspan in space. Bigger is always better when it comes to cages and aviaries.

The right spot
Do not leave a bird cage in a draught and make sure it is never in full sunlight.

The right bowl
Small birds are fine using small plastic feeding and water bowls, but parrots and other large birds tend to chew them up and toss them around. Buy china or steel bowls that can be attached to the cage.

Clean cage
Do not use detergents when cleaning out a bird cage: hot water is adequate.

Smooth bath
If birds slip in the bird bath, place a piece of foam rubber on the bottom.

Spoil a canary
Canaries love pear or apple, and a piece of hard-boiled egg is an extra-special treat.

Sing for me
For canaries to sing, you need both a male and a female.

Poisonous for birds:
- Chocolate
- Avocado pear
- Mushrooms
- Too much onion
- The seeds of apples and pears
- Apricot stones

Hot days

Give parakeets and parrots a shower on very hot days by spraying them with a pot-plant spray. Make sure there is a draught-free spot for them to dry off.

Hyperactive parrot

A hyperactive parrot is usually getting too little calcium. Reduce the vitamin supplements sprinkled on seed and fruit and rather add calcium to his drinking water. Also get your parrot a cuttlebone. Not only is it rich in calcium, but it also sharpens the parrot's beak and nails.

How to keep happy chickens

- Send chickens out into the garden in the morning and put them back into their coop at night. Keep their food and water dishes full and collect the eggs regularly.
- When keeping chickens for the first time, keep them in their coop for a couple of weeks before letting them loose in the garden. They should then return to the coop by themselves at night and, if you provide a comfortable place to roost, they will lay their eggs there.
- An old grass catcher from a lawnmower makes a cosy nest and is also conveniently portable.
- Make sure the chicken coop offers sufficient protection from the sun and rain.
- It is best to shut chickens away at night because stray cats might kill them.
- If your chickens live in a coop, make sure they have enough clean water and a balanced diet. In addition to feed of mixed grains and seeds, a chicken needs 20 g green feed a day – organic kitchen waste and leftover food are favourites.

Notes

Notes

house PLANTS

13

The secret to happy house plants

For lush, healthy house plants you need more than just green fingers: you need to be willing to care for your plants regularly.

13.1 POT PLANTS

Dusty leaves

Wipe the dusty leaves of pot plants with a mixture of water and a little milk on a cloth. Wipe the leaves dry afterwards.

Banana peel

Use the inside of a banana peel to clean plant leaves and it will feed the plant at the same time.

Neglected pot plants

Move plants that tend to be neglected to a new position where they will be easier to look after.

Fertiliser for pot plants

Finely crushed egg shells and tea leaves or coffee grounds are good for feeding pot plants.

Clay granules key to success

Always put a good layer of hydro clay granules at the bottom of the pot and water well. Then add the plant and potting soil, and top with clay granules. The granules provide good drainage and make more water available to a pot plant over a longer period.

Filter bags for drainage

Place a paper filter bag for a coffee machine at the bottom of the pot to improve the drainage without the soil falling out.

Hardened potting soil

If the soil in the pot has become hard and unyielding, it means it is too wet. Add some sand or peat moss.

Mould on top

Mould on top of potting soil is harmless, but may look unsightly. Replace the top layer of soil and give the plant less water.

Sodden potting soil

Soil that is continuously wet is not draining properly, and pot plants will rot in it. You will need to replace the soil at the bottom of the pot. When doing so, add a coarse material that encourages drainage, such as clay granules, gravel or polystyrene balls.

If the soil in the pot has become hard and unyielding, it means it is too wet. Add some sand or peat moss.

Going on holiday?

Place porous pots in large basins with moist peat moss or sphagnum moss from a renewable source. The pots will absorb moisture through the sides as well and will remain moist for longer in the large basin.

Wool to water plants

Place a ball of wool in a bucket of water and put the end of the wool in the pot-plant soil. Position the bucket slightly higher than the pot plant and water will move from the bucket to the plant through the wool. The thicker the wool, the more water the pot plant will receive.

Drainage hole

Every pot in which you plant a pot plant needs a drainage hole in the bottom. If you are loathe to drill a hole in a particular pot, you can still use it if you put about 10 cm of clay granules in the bottom and then place the pot plant in it in its original plastic container. Remember to prune the roots of the plant every year.

Leaves turning green

If the leaves of a plant with coloured leaves turn green, the plant is not getting enough light. Move the plant to a spot that is brighter or that gets light for longer every day.

Red cactus

If a cactus in a pot starts to change colour, it is probably getting too much direct sunlight.

Yellow leaves

If the fully grown leaves of a ficus or delicious monster turn yellow, they are either not getting enough light or not enough carbon dioxide. Also ensure that you are not watering them too much.

Wilted plants

Plants that droop despite receiving enough water, are probably standing in too hot a spot. This is more likely to happen when a plant is left on a windowsill in the afternoon sun.

Cyclamen

A cyclamen that does not flower is probably too hot.

Bromelia

If your bromelia does not flower, place the pot in a see-through plastic bag along with a few apples. Close the bag tightly and leave for at least a week. The apples give off ethylene, which encourages bromelias to bloom.

Meths for ferns

Every three months, sprinkle 10 ml methylated spirits on the ground around a fern to stimulate lush growth.

Keep aphids away

Stick a number of matches with sulfur heads into the soil around a pot plant that is infested with aphids. Make sure that the match heads just touch the ground. The sulfur will dissolve in the moisture in the soil, and the aphids will leave.

Test strips

Test the acidity or alkalinity of your pot plants with test strips available from nurseries. Deficiencies are easy to right with liquid plant foods.

Check the pots

It is a good idea to check all your pot plants every year or two to see whether the roots need pruning and whether the plant needs a bigger pot.

Plastic lids

Place old plastic lids under pot plants in the house.

Tinfoil for pots and planters

Line iron and wooden planters with tinfoil to prevent the soil coming into direct contact with the pot. Also line the drainage holes. Doing this helps pots last much longer.

Use rubbish bins when moving

Place pot plants in your rubbish bins when moving house and there will be far less mess at the other end.

Make your own plant food

Keep seaweed and bamboo in a bucket of water, and use the water for your pot plants. Remember to change the water in the seaweed brew every ten days. It is also very good for vegetable gardens, herb gardens and young seedlings because it does not burn plants and can never be given in too strong a dose.

13.2 FLOWERS

Pick flowers early

When picking flowers for the vase, pick them early in the morning or on a cloudy day, before they start to lose moisture. Cut the stems at an angle and keep a bucket of water to hand to store the flowers as you pick them.

When arranging fewer than 15 blooms in a vase, use an odd number for a more harmonious effect.

Roses

- To keep roses looking good for longer in a vase, cut off the thorns, strip off any leaves that are below the water line in the vase, and cut the stems diagonally. Place the roses in ice-cold water in which a little sugar has been dissolved. If the roses are looking tired after a few days, add an aspirin to the water. Remember to replace the water with cold, fresh water regularly.
- You can also place wilted roses, bloom and all, into a cold bath to refresh them.

Cut under water

Cut the stems of blooms under water to prevent air entering the stems.

Tulips

Add a dash of vodka to the water when arranging a vaseful of tulips, to prevent the stems drooping. If the heads start to hang down, make a pinprick hole just below the flower head.

Cut flowers

Always cut a piece off the bottom of the stem, even if the flowers are ready to put in a vase. Add a little bleach to the water and replace the water after a week, when you should also cut another piece off the bottom of the stems.

Revitalise cut blooms

Revive cut flowers by placing the stems in boiling water. By the time the water has cooled the blooms will be upright again. Then cut the ends off the stems and arrange in fresh, cold water.

Porous flowerpot

Rub the inside of a porous flowerpot with candle wax or paraffin to make it watertight.

Good composition

When arranging fewer than 15 blooms in a vase, use an odd number for a more harmonious effect.

Prevent stains

If you are worried about an expensive glass vase becoming stained on the bottom, place a piece of cotton wool in the vase before pouring in the water. If the glass is transparent, use some crumpled cellophane.

Transporting bouquets

Transport bouquets in a cooler box with ice packs.

Old silk flowers

Rejuvenate old silk flowers by rinsing them out in fabric softener and drying with a hairdryer.

Vases that scratch the table

Attach pretty puffy stickers or sticking to the base of your vases if you are worried about the surface getting scratched.

Preserve leaves and flowers

- Place autumn leaves in 2 cm of a water and glycerine solution, and leave to stand until all the liquid has been absorbed. The leaves can then be used in dry arrangements for months.
- Preserve proteas and hydrangeas using the same method.

Short stems
If you have cut the stems of flowers too short, lengthen them using drinking straws.

Marbles to the rescue
If you are struggling with a flower arrangement and do not have any florist's oasis to hand, fill the base of the vase to one-third with marbles.

Recycle oasis
Use a piece of oasis more than once by wrapping it in tinfoil.

Elastic for arums
Tie elastic bands around the bottom of the stems of fleshy plants, such as arum lilies and agapanthus, to stop the stems opening and curling up.

Pink proteas
To help pink proteas keep their colour for longer, add pink food colouring to the water.

Golden rules of flower arranging
- Use a plain vase if you want the flowers to be the centre of attention.
- A single rose in a vase is more beautiful than two.
- The stems of the blooms must not cross above the top of the vase.
- The heaviest blooms and leaves should be at the bottom of your arrangement.

Notes

the GARDEN

14

The truth about weeds

The best way to tell the difference between a useful plant and a weed is to give it a tug. If it comes out easily, it is a useful plant!

14.1 PATHWAYS AND PAVING

Calculate quantities

Calculate how many pavers or stones you need for a particular project by working out how much you need per square metre. Then multiply the number of units by the total number of square metres. Buy a few extra pavers or tiles to replace those that get broken.

Calculate the depth

Paving laid on soft ground will subside over time. You therefore need to dig out the topsoil until you reach the hard subsoil. The depth of the foundation is determined by and calculated according to the quantity and type of material (geotextile or coarse builder's rubble) to be used, as well as a 10 cm layer of sand to level the surface and, finally, the height of the paver or tile. A further 10 cm must be allowed for a cement mixture, if this is going to be used.

Firm foundation for tiles

- The more unstable the subsoil, the thicker the foundation must be.
- The thinner the tile, the heavier and firmer the foundation must be.
- The greater the traffic and the heavier the traffic the path will carry, the firmer the foundation must be.

Avoid damp problems

Remember that paving should slope away from the house to prevent problems such as standing water and resulting rising damp.

Wet saw

When cutting pavers or tiles with a wet saw, mark the cutting lines with a permanent marker so that the water does not erase your marks.

Round patio

When building a round or arched terrace, lay the stones row by row from the outside inwards. Draw a circle from the midpoint using a stick and twine to determine the position of the outside edge. The closer you get to the centre of the circle, the bigger the gaps between the stones will become. Fill the last gap with a rectangular piece of stone.

14.2 OUTDOOR TOYS

Trampoline safety

A trampoline on a frame must always stand on soft ground or grass. On a hard surface a trampoline will start to move about when in use. It is also safer to position a trampoline on a soft surface in case someone comes off it.

Jungle gyms

- If children can fall further than a metre from a jungle gym, the surface on which it stands must be impact-absorbing. Use at least 50 cm of river sand or wood chips.
- If children are able to fall less than one metre, grass is adequate.

Swings

When setting up a swing, make the gap between the ropes wider at the top than at the bottom so that it is more difficult for the swing to become twisted. If it does become twisted, a swing set up like this will be easier to untwist.

Sand pit

Rake the sand in the sand pit every day to get air to circulate through it and to look for lost toys. Unpleasant bugs can breed in a wet sand pit, so make sure that the sand remains dry at all times. To prevent cats using it as a toilet, cover a sand pit with a piece of tightly woven shade cloth cut to size.

Test sand-pit sand

- Test sand by putting a tablespoon of it into a glass of water and stirring. If the sand sinks to the bottom and the water remains clear, the sand is clean. If the water remains cloudy, the sand is not suitable for a sand pit.
- If you have no alternative, wash the sand. Sift the sand and then spray it with a household disinfectant diluted with water.

When setting up a swing, make the gap between the ropes wider at the top than at the bottom so that it is more difficult for the swing to become twisted.

Paddling pool

Cover a paddling pool with a nylon car cover when not in use. Sew elastic around the edges of the cover so that it is easy to pull on and off. If you do not replace the water regularly, you will need to use a chlorine product to keep it clean.

Chlorine for the pool

Chlorine works best if you put it in the pool in the evening, after the sun has set.

Swimming pools and drought

- If you are no longer permitted to top up your pool, it is advisable to reduce the chlorine level in the pool by adding less chlorine. By removing the cover from the pool, the sun will also help with this. Use swimming-pool water to water precious plants.
- Find out how much water must remain in the swimming pool for it not to become damaged structurally.

14.3 GARDEN TOOLS AND EQUIPMENT

Choose garden tools carefully

- The most expensive garden equipment is not necessarily the best. Figure out exactly what you want to do with it before going out and buying anything. Industrial gardening equipment and farm tools are often heavy and awkward to use, and far too big for a small garden.
- However, do invest in a good pair of pruning shears with blades that can be sharpened when they become blunt. Maintain garden equipment well and it will give you many years of good service.

Hosepipe storage

Store a hosepipe by winding it around an old wheel rim.

Extra-long hosepipe

A long hosepipe can be stored in an old tyre.

Instant sprinkler

Find a one-litre plastic bottle with a top that fits snugly on the hosepipe. Make holes in one side of the bottle using a hot nail, and use it as a temporary sprinkler head.

Tool maintenance

- Sharpen a spade or hoe with a small file, filing in the direction of the digging side. Pruning shears can be filed using a diamond file.
- Rub a little oil on the blades, screws and bolts of garden equipment to prevent rust.

Clean shears

Always clean pruning shears with methylated spirits or ethyl alcohol after use to prevent the spread of plant diseases in your garden.

Remove rust

Scrub rusted tools with a wire brush and then clean using a rust remover. Soak stubborn rust spots in paraffin for a while before scouring.

A rake with reach

Attach a longer handle to a children's rake so that you can rake hard-to-reach spots under shrubs, for example.

Patch a hosepipe

Holes in a hosepipe can be patched with strips cut from an inner tube. Secure with wire.

Prevent rust in wheelbarrows

Turn a wheelbarrow upside down or stand it upright against a wall when not in use to prevent water accumulating in it, leading to rust.

Wooden storage bench

Build a wooden storage box for your garden tools that doubles as seating.

14.4 GARDENING TIPS

Water-wise gardening

Plant indigenous plants if you want to reduce the amount of water your garden needs. Most indigenous plants are hardy and can survive for longer in drought conditions.

Do your homework

Never set off for the nursery or garden shop unprepared. Impulse purchases are usually expensive, and often the plants will not flourish in your garden.

How to make a compost heap

1. Start with a 10 cm layer of dried leaves at the bottom of the heap. Top with 2,5 cm good-quality garden soil, with 5 cm cut grass on top. Then alternate the layers of green and brown material. Wet the heap as you go – it should feel as damp as a squeezed-out sponge.
2. You will need a lot of material to build a compost heap that will generate enough heat to kill pathogenic organisms and undesirable seeds in the compost, so make sure that you collect enough material beforehand. Dig the heap over as soon as you feel that the heat inside is dropping (after about 10 to 14 days), and bury coffee grounds, egg shells and other vegetable scraps from the kitchen in it.
3. After that, dig the compost heap over every two weeks and dampen if necessary. The compost is ready when you no longer recognise individual pieces of plant matter.

Turbo compost

Chicken droppings, horse dung or any other animal manure (except from dogs and cats) will give a compost heap a boost and help generate more heat.

Sun protection

In very hot weather, the compost heap can be covered with a piece of old carpet or shade cloth to reduce evaporation.

Cut up plant material

The finer the plant material you use, the finer the texture of the compost will be. Lay twigs and other garden refuse on the lawn (brown and green material mixed) and go over it with the lawnmower on its highest setting. This will chop up the material finely and you can simply toss it straight onto the compost heap from the grass box.

Test compost

- Keep your compost heap damp during dry months, but it must never become too wet. If you squeeze a small amount of the compost in your hand and it runs like mud, it is too wet.
- If the heap smells nasty and attracts flies, it is also probably too wet. Turn it over and mix with brown material.

Brew liquid manure

- Plants are able to absorb manure more easily when it is liquid. Make your own liquid manure by filling a plastic container (not metal) with one-third cow dung, sheep dung, horse dung or chicken droppings, and two-thirds water. Stir the mixture until the dung has dissolved in the water. Cover the container and leave to brew in a cool place for six to eight weeks. It does not smell pleasant, but the smell dissipates quickly after being applied.
- If you want to dispense the mixture using a watering can with a fine rose, place the dung in a net vegetable bag and use it like a tea bag. Swirl it around in the container about once a week. Dilute the mixture with water in a ratio of 1:5 before using it on plants.
- Apply manure in the evening after sunset or early in the morning before sunrise because ultraviolet rays will destroy desirable micro-organisms in the manure. Sprinkle the mixture on the ground around plants and if you want to apply it to the foliage, dilute it further in a ratio of 1:10.

Tea leaves

Tea leaves make excellent mulch for ferns. Do not smother the roots of the plants by applying the tea leaves directly to them; rather dig the tea leaves gently into the soil.

Coffee grounds

Coffee grounds make a very effective addition to compost, and earthworms are mad about them. Also dig coffee grounds into your garden in places where the plants require acidic soil.

Never set off for the nursery or garden shop unprepared. Impulse purchases are usually expensive, and often the plants will not flourish in your garden.

Iron for plants

Bury pieces of old steel wool with plants, such as hydrangeas, that need iron.

Buy new seed

Check seed packets to see whether the seed is an F1 hybrid. This means the seed has been produced by crossing two different types of seed. It is not worth harvesting the seed of these plants because the new seedlings will not have the characteristics of the parent plant. Rather buy new seed every year, or buy seed from a supplier that does not pollinate in a controlled environment.

Scatter seed

Do not scatter the seed straight from the packet. Rather pour a little at a time into the palm of your hand and scatter it gently using your thumb and index finger. If the seed is very fine, mix it with sand first or pour it into an empty spice bottle or sugar shaker and scatter it from there.

Stop beds drying out

To stop seed beds drying out, lay newspaper or sacking over the beds, but make sure they still get enough light. Also ensure that snails do not make themselves at home under the sacking. Once the seedlings have more than three leaves, remove the cover.

Home-made garden soil

1. Place damp soil from the garden or old potting soil in an oven bag (the kind you use for roasting chicken).
2. Insert an ovenproof thermometer into the bag and tie it securely.
3. Place the bag of soil on a baking sheet in an oven preheated to 120 °C.

4. When the soil reaches 100 °C, reduce the oven temperature to 100 °C and bake the soil for half an hour at this temperature. If the soil gets hotter than 100 °C its structure is altered and you will not be able to use it.
5. Remove from the oven and leave to cool completely before using it.
6. Mix equal quantities of building sand, peat and the sterilised soil. The sand can also be replaced with vermiculite or perlite, both of which must be soaked in water beforehand.
7. Warning: baked soil has a strong smell, so open the windows before you start baking.

Help from the moles

Instead of sterilising soil to make your own garden soil, scoop up earth from fresh molehills and use as is. The earth comes from deep under the ground and will be free of plant diseases.

Help seedlings acclimatise

Before seedlings that have been propagated indoors can be replanted outside, they must gradually get used to being outside. Place the seedling trays outside for part of the day, but avoid direct sun initially. Bring them back inside a little later each day and after a week you will be able to plant them out.

Harvesting seed

Harvest seed only from healthy plants, as sick plants produce sick seed. Store the seed in paper bags or containers in a cool, dry place. Seed that gets too hot will not sprout.

Seed containers

Store each type of seed in a separate container and mark each container clearly. Empty soup and sauce packets made of foil are ideal for storing seed.

Making softwood cuttings

1. A cutting can be 5–15 cm long, depending on the size of the parent plant. Make a straight cut approximately 5–10 cm from the uppermost leaves on the stem. Remove the bottom leaves so that the stem is bare at the bottom. Plant the cutting in such a way that the part where the bottom leaves were is covered with soil.

2. Once softwood cuttings have been planted, keep them damp at all times but ensure the drainage is very good because cuttings rot easily. Once cuttings have a sound root system they can be planted out.

Greenhouse for cuttings

To keep cuttings warm and moist, make a miniature greenhouse by sticking four sticks in the pot and stretching a clear plastic bag over them. Close the bag in such a way that a small amount of air is still able to circulate. Do not place the cuttings in full sunlight.

Making hardwood cuttings

1. A hardwood cutting must be approximately 20–30 cm long and about 0,5–1,5 cm thick.
2. Make the cutting underneath the branch just below a node, and on the top of the branch approximately 2 cm above a node.
3. Remove the leaves from the bottom two-thirds.
4. Plant the cuttings straight into the ground in a pot of soil sold specifically for this purpose.
5. Position the cutting so that the place where the leaves were removed is below the surface.

Successful cuttings

To achieve the greatest success with both hardwood and softwood cuttings, dip the cut end into growth hormone (powder or liquid) before planting.

Weeds

Use an out-of-service apple corer from the kitchen to remove weeds from the ground. Push the corer into the ground, twist and pull out the weed.

Use an out-of-service apple corer from the kitchen to remove weeds from the ground.

When transplanting a mature tree, tie a rope to a north-facing branch.

Useful toilet rolls

Push empty cardboard toilet roll tubes over seedlings that are being threatened by cut worms. Only the edge of the roll should be visible above the ground. The roll will protect the plant's roots.

Bulbs for next season

In order to bloom again next year, the bulb must continue growing after flowering in order to gather its strength. Rather let the plant die back on its own.

Bulb storage

Place bulbs in egg boxes or in a pillowcase and store in a cool, dry place.

Hint of nostalgia

Catch water under the garden tap in an old-fashioned bucket or earthenware pot planted with mint, which will thrive there.

Transplanting a tree

When transplanting a mature tree, tie a rope to a north-facing branch. The branch with the rope must point in the same direction when the tree is in its new position.

Fish pond

Try to establish a balanced ecology in a fish pond as quickly as possible to minimise potential problems. Chemicals have only a temporary effect. Plant oxygen-producing plants, install a good-quality filter and pump, and remove old plants. Water also evaporates quickly from a fish pond, so top it up regularly.

Training runners

Fill the foot of a stocking with small stones and tie it to a runner you want to train it in a particular direction. Throw the stocking over the wall or trellis so that the runner is pulled in the right direction.

Bone-dry lawn

- Spike holes in an extremely dry lawn before watering it to stop the water simply running off the hard ground.
- In dry regions, the edge of the lawn should be 3–5 cm higher than the middle, a difference that should be virtually invisible to the naked eye. This will stop the water running away, giving it a chance to soak into the grass.

Grass in cracks

- Sprinkle salt into the cracks in a path or paving to stop grass growing in them. Salt is better for the environment than weed or grass killer.
- On a sunny day, spray neat vinegar on weeds that are coming up in the paving. Those that are not killed outright by the vinegar will be finished off by the sun.

Ground cover

Plant ground cover instead of grass on very steep inclines and other areas that will be difficult to mow.

Keep grass alive

Grass that is cut too short is likely to die off. The grass will not be able to manufacture food and the roots will be exposed to the sun. Try not to cut off more than a third of the blade of grass.

Attract birds to your garden

- Birds bring life to a garden. If they feel at home, other small creatures are likely to follow.
- Hang up bird houses and feeders, and put out extra food.
- Roll a pine cone in peanut butter and then in bird seed. Hang the cone in your garden.
- Fill net vegetable bags with unshelled peanuts and hang them over the branches of trees.
- Make seed cakes by melting animal fat and stirring bird seed through it. Leave the fat to set in a tin or mould and keep the cakes in the

Plant ground cover instead of grass on very steep inclines and areas that will be difficult to mow.

fridge until you need them. Hang a seed cake in a tree in a net vegetable bag, or push it firmly into a fork in the branches. You could also place them on a feeding platform or in a bird feeder. Warning: margarine is not animal fat and will make the birds sick.

- Build a wooden feeding platform that you can hang from a branch or place on a pole. Use the platform to offer garden birds a variety of fruit and pieces of cheese, bread and bacon every day.

14.5 VEGETABLE GARDEN

Recipe for success

The secret is to start small – you can only enjoy a vegetable garden if you can control it! If you make a success of your small garden, you can always add a bit more next year. Choose plants that are easy to grow and produce good crops, such as tomatoes, strawberries, carrots and various types of lettuce.

What size pot for veggies?

- Plant a cherry tomato plant in a 14 cm pot.
- Plant one head of lettuce in a 16 cm pot.
- Plant garlic and onions in a 25 cm pot.
- Plant carrots in a 35 cm pot.
- Plant a pumpkin in a 35 cm pot and train the runners up a trellis.
- Plant a miniature fruit tree in a large pot. Peaches, apricots, lemons and apples usually do well. Even though such a tree will not grow to more than 1,5 metres tall, it will produce more than enough fruit.

HERBS

Herb garden in a hurry

Buy a bag of potting soil from the nursery and lay it flat in a sunny spot. Make a cross in the plastic using a sharp knife and plant the herbs right there in the bag. Water the plants regularly and before you know it the bag will be overgrown with herbs.

Edible flowers

- The flowers of culinary herbs are edible: try the blossoms of basil, borage, chives, coriander, garlic, lavender, marjoram, rosemary and thyme.
- These flowers are also edible: anise hyssop, chrysanthemums, marigolds, nasturtiums, pansies, pumpkin and roses.
- Warning: ensure that the plants have not been sprayed with poison.

Herb seedlings in a pot

Decide which herbs you want to plant, then choose a container that is wide and deep enough to allow the seedlings to grow to maturity in it. Depending on the type of herbs you plant, you should get six seedlings in a 30 cm container. If your pots are bigger, divide the plants and spread them over the entire area.

Plant a miniature fruit tree in a large pot. Peaches, apricots, lemons and apples usually do well.

Sun or shade?

- If the container will get plenty of sun, including hot afternoon sun, choose from thyme, origanum, coriander, French lavender, bay, basil, lemon verbena, dill, parsley, chives, rosemary and sage.
- For a spot that gets less sun, choose from parsley, spearmint, mint, chives, violets, borage and lemon balm.

Plant for contrast

Plant large and small herbs together in a container for maximum effect.

- *Small herbs:* parsley, hives, origanum, peppermint, spearmint, thyme.
- *Medium-sized herbs*: marjoram, basil, tarragon, savory, mint, coriander, lemon grass.
- *Large herbs:* rosemary, lavender, sage, lemon verbena, pineapple sage, curry plant, bay (bay grows very slowly but eventually becomes a tree).

Sugared violets

- Brush freshly picked violets with lightly beaten egg white and sprinkle an even coating of caster sugar over them. Dry in a cool oven with the door open for 10–15 minutes, then store in an airtight container. Use to decorate cakes and cupcakes.
- Experiment with rose petals and other edible flowers from the garden.

Herbal tea

- Always use a china teapot, as metal ones can affect the taste.
- Brew a tea using two tablespoons fresh herbs or one tablespoon dried herbs for every cup of water, plus one or two extra spoonfuls of fresh and one extra spoonful of dried herbs to taste for the pot.

- Pour the boiling water over the herbs in the teapot and leave to brew for at least five minutes. Pour the tea through a tea strainer.
- The following, among others, are suitable for making tea: anise, chamomile, ginger root, lavender, mint, peppermint, lemon balm (*Melissa officinalis*), renosterbos, lemon grass.

14.6 PESTS

COCKROACHES

Death by icing sugar

- Combine equal quantities gypsum and icing sugar, place in containers and leave them where the cockroaches are fond of lurking. The gypsum will solidify their guts and kill them.
- Borax and icing sugar also work.

Fragrance deterrents

Scatter Epsom salts, sage sprigs, banana peels, khaki bush, cloves or lavender oil on shelves to keep cockroaches away.

ANTS

Dust them out

Sprinkle cayenne pepper, baby powder or powdered cloves in the path of ants.

Ants in a tree

Tie a cloth soaked in paraffin around a fruit tree to keep the ants away.

Start at the source

The best place to deal with ants is in their nest. Pour boiling water into an ant nest regularly, or sprinkle abrasive powder or coffee grounds around it.

MOLES

Think twice about driving moles from your garden: they aerate the soil and eat snails and the larvae of insect pests. If you really want to get rid of a mole, push garlic into as many parts of the tunnels as you can reach, and close up the holes. You can also remove the bottom from a plastic cooldrink bottle and push the bottle into the hole until only the open top is sticking out. The whistling caused by the wind blowing over the top of the bottle will soon have the mole packing its bags.

MICE AND RATS

Avoid using single-dose poisons and rather go for multiple-dose ones that the rodent must eat for at least four consecutive days. A multiple-dose agent poses less of a danger to pets and to birds of prey that might eat the dead rodent. Single-dose poisons will poison the next animal in the food chain too.

Close mouse holes by sprinkling a few drops of peppermint oil in the hole and stuffing steel wool into it.

Rodent infestations

If there is a severe infestation of rats, a poison containing an anticoagulant, such as Racumin Paste, which causes death by internal bleeding, is recommended. However, this is a dangerous poison that must be handled very carefully.

Mouse traps

Wear rubber gloves when setting mouse traps so that your scent does not remain on the trap. Put out traps for a few days just to get the mice used to them.

Drown mice

Fill a drum with water and scatter enough sunflower seeds on the water to completely cover the surface. Mice will think it is food, jump in and drown.

Mouse holes

Close mouse holes by sprinkling a few drops of peppermint oil in the hole and stuffing steel wool into it. You could also dip a cork in turpentine and push it into the hole.

MOSQUITOES

Temporary mosquito net

Attach a piece of shade cloth to a window with reusable putty to act as a temporary mosquito net.

Plant herbs such as basil, rosemary, mint as well as lavender near windows and doors to deter flies.

Find where they breed

Get rid of containers and pools of stagnant water in which mosquitoes can breed. Replace your pets' water every day and put lids on water tanks.

Candles and fragrance

Buy or make citronella candles to burn when you are outside in the garden. You could also put a few drops of eucalyptus oil on a piece of cotton wool on your bedside table, and place sprigs of mint on your pillow.

KEEPING SNAILS AT BAY

Copper wire

If snails are going after your pot plants, tie copper wire around the pots. The wire will give the snails a slight shock.

A glass of beer

- Place containers of beer with smooth, steep sides among your plants. Snails cannot resist beer and will drown in it because they are unable to get out of the container.
- Soak a piece of sacking in beer and place it flat on the ground among the plants. The snails will crawl under the sack at night to get to the beer. In the morning you can harvest them for your chickens!

Natural pest control

- Planting herbs among other plants will help control garden pests. Plant lavender with roses, and marigolds (*Tagetes erecta*) among vegetables. A row of garlic or chives at the edge of a flower bed will help keep pests away.
- Also plant the indigenous wild garlic *Tulbaghia violacea*. Not only will you have the pleasure of enjoying the beautiful flowers, but densely planted, it is also effective at stopping grass spreading into beds.

Termites and borer beetle

- These days it is compulsory for the wood in houses to be treated for borer beetle and termites, and you should not be troubled by them if your house is a new one. However, examine the wood in old houses for signs of beetle activity and call in the professionals to deal with infested wood.
- Open up termite holes and pour approximately 15 ml swimming-pool chorine into the tunnel. The termites will carry the granules into the nest, where it is damp. The granules will be converted into gas, which kills the termites.

Fish moths

Fish moths are discussed in Chapter 5, The Bedroom (see page 46).

Flies

Plant herbs such as basil, rosemary, mint and lavender near windows and doors to deter flies.

FLEAS

Light solution

Being plagued by fleas even though you do not have pets? Place a burning candle in a dish or bowl of water with a spoonful of dishwashing liquid and a little salad dressing, and put the dish on the carpet. Fleas will jump towards the light and drown in the water. Ensure that the dish is large enough for the flame to be extinguished if the candle falls over during the night.

Khaki bush

Steep khaki bush in boiling water and spray the brew onto the walls of outbuildings.

Herbs to try

Place mint under mats and stuff pets' cushions with a mixture of lavender, cedarwood shavings and rosemary.

Feathered pests

- Old-fashioned scarecrows are charming and often very effective. To make your own, build a frame from twigs and rope, then dress your figure in old clothes. Use a flowerpot or pumpkin for the head. Paint a face on the pot and plant grass in it to look like hair once it grows.
- Make a sun catcher from old CDs and hang it from a branch. The sun reflecting off the discs will scare away the birds.
- Tie bottles to twine in a tree so that the bottles tinkle against each other when the wind blows.

Beware of insecticides

Insecticides should be used with caution. Remember that for every insect pest they kill, they will also kill an insect that is beneficial to the garden. The best approach is to remove insect pests in a targeted way.

Protect roses

Protect your roses against a variety of pests by sterilising the ground around each rose bush in the autumn. Use a mixture of 10–15 ml Jeyes Fluid diluted in 5 litres of water.

Solution for general garden pests

Steep a packet of pipe tobacco in three litres of hot water and spray insect-infested plants with this brew. Add a few drops of liquid soap to the mixture as a surfactant.

Garlic spray for aphids

Mix 100 g finely chopped garlic, two tablespoons paraffin, 10 g green household soap and 600 ml water and use on aphids and caterpillars.

Notes

the GREAT OUTDOORS 15

Take it with you

Leave only your footprints at the places you go to relax outdoors.

Clean the braai grid

Rub the braai grid with half an onion or half a lemon once it has become hot on the fire. This also gives the meat a good flavour.

Light a fire

As an alternative to conventional fire lighters, pour old cooking oil into a cardboard egg box. Place the box on the bottom of the braai and build your fire around it.

Used tea bags as fire lighters

Leave used tea bags to dry out completely before dipping them in melted candlewax. Allow the wax to set again before using the bags as lighters.

Rosemary for flavour

Toss a couple of sprigs of rosemary on the coals to give your meat a wonderful flavour.

Buy good-quality wood

Quality wood is essential for a successful braai. Camel thorn, sicklewood, hard wood (*hardehout*) and vine stumps are good. Tamboti, seringa and oleander give off toxic fumes and are not suitable.

Camping checklist

- Draw up a standard camping checklist on the computer that you can use every holiday, and update it when necessary. Then before you start packing, print out a copy of the list. The internet has many examples of such lists that will serve as a good starting point when compiling yours.
- You could also buy a camping trunk in which you keep essential camping equipment permanently. Then, if on a Friday afternoon you decide to go camping for the weekend, the trunk is packed and ready to go.

Reference guide

Buy a file with plastic pockets in which to keep the information on your caravan and camping equipment. You can also keep information on campsites, reservation numbers, maps and other documents in this file.

Camping furniture

When buying camping furniture, remember that the higher a chair the easier it will be to get up out of it. Also consider that the height of your chairs and table should be in proportion in order to be comfortable. Buy a table with adjustable legs to ensure it is always level.

Stop the tent blowing away

If you are worried about your tent or groundsheet blowing away, fill a few plastic milk bottles with sand and attach them to the canvas with rope (at least one at each corner). The sand anchors are also useful when the ground is too hard to knock in a peg.

Dirty canvas

If a large groundsheet is very dirty after a camping trip, throw it in the swimming pool. The sheet will not sink to the bottom and will come out clean again.

Keep cables out the way

Attach shower curtain hooks to the outside of your stoep tent and lead the cables through them. This will keep loose cables out from under everyone's feet.

Picnic blanket

Buy a pretty plastic tablecloth and sew it to the back of a soft blanket to make the perfect waterproof picnic blanket.

Caravan gas canisters

Always ensure that the gas canisters for your caravan are easily accessible so that they can be removed quickly in the event of a fire.

Packing tip

Save space on camping trips by taking along plastic crates that can be packed flat. Pack all your gear in plastic bags and transport it like that. Only reassemble the crates when you want to use them in the tent.

Rub the braai grid with half an onion or half a lemon once it has become hot on the fire. This also gives the meat a good flavour.

More than one key
Have a caravan key cut for every member of the family. There is nothing more annoying than arriving back at the campsite to find the caravan locked and no one home.

Foil to the rescue
Oven foil is essential when camping. It can be used to cook vegetables and fish on the fire, to wrap potatoes before placing them among the coals, for baking bananas with marshmallows, and for cooking a batch of flapjacks over the coals.

Prepare hiking boots
Apply a thick layer of petroleum jelly to hiking boots you want to walk in, while heating them with a hairdryer. The leather will become supple and waterproof.

Plastic poncho
Always take a plastic poncho when you go hiking. Ponchos fold up very small and have many uses. You can even tie one over your tent as extra protection from heavy rain.

Refuse bags for water
Tie black refuse bags over your shoes and legs if you want to get to the other side of a river and stay dry.

Humid conditions
If you are on a hike in very hot and humid conditions and want to wash your clothes even though you know they will not dry because the air is too damp, simply wash your clothes as soon as you arrive at camp and put them on again wet. Not only will your clothes be clean, but they will also cool you down.

Plastic bag as wash basin
Wash camping clothes in the plastic bag in which you originally packed them.

Keep the bugs out
Pull your hiking socks over your boots at night to make sure no unwelcome critters sneak into your boots.

Matches that work

Dip matches in varnish if you want to be sure they will light when damp.

Pine time

When camping in the vicinity of pine trees, you can use some of their resin to make your fire burn better. Make a small notch in the trunk of the tree and catch the resin on a tissue or piece of cotton wool. Add the tissue or cotton wool to the fire. The resin in dry pine cones will also encourage a fire to burn.

Campsite dangers

- The biggest danger when camping in the bush is an unexpected natural disaster. Look for a site that is on raised ground, rather than in a dip. Be especially careful to avoid dry river beds through which the river might flow unexpectedly. If the weather is very hot and dry, choose an open spot in a wooded area and preferably as far away as possible from trees that burn easily, such as eucalyptus and pines.
- Familiarise yourselves with the area and work out an escape route.

Holiday time

- Have your car serviced before you go on holiday.
- Always maintain a safe following distance and increase it during inclement weather.
- Take a rest after every 200 km.

Book your own international holiday

Booking your own holiday overseas on the internet can save you a lot of money, but there are many pitfalls to be aware of. Make sure you book with a reputable airline, and find out from reliable sources whether you require a visa. Also check that your passport is valid for long enough after your return. If you book a very cheap flight, make provision for possible delays and allow enough time for connecting flights. Read as many ratings and comments by previous guests at hotels and guesthouses as possible before making a booking on the internet.

How to holiday on a budget

- Decide on a fixed daily budget and stick to it.
- Book accommodation out of peak holiday season.

- Eat where the locals do. When in Europe, remember the rule: the closer to water or a major tourist attraction you eat, the more you are going to pay.
- Adjust your spending pattern. Buy food at a supermarket or market and prepare it yourself, rather than eating every meal in a restaurant.
- Ensure you have control over your cellphone costs and banking charges.

Packing tips

- Put everything you plan to take with you next to your suitcase. Recall from previous trips what you packed and never wore, then remove those items from the pile.
- Look at the weather forecast for where you are going.
- Choose clothes in a particular range of colours so that you can mix and match.
- Dispense toiletries such as shampoo into smaller plastic bottles, or buy small travel sizes.
- Trousers will crease less if you roll them up instead of laying them flat in your suitcase.
- You can also roll a few items of clothing together to prevent creases.
- Wear your heaviest shoes and coat when travelling to save space in your suitcase.
- Take a facecloth, as many budget hotels do not provide one.

Shoe covers

Use old socks as shoe covers for your trip.

Notes

Mbeya
Eastern
Luangwa
Mbala
Senga Hill
Chipasanse
Mpulungu
Kayambi
Nondo
Kiakalamu
Kabongo
Luanza
Mitwaba
Lusinga
Sampwe
Kundelungu
Kundelungu National Park
Mamba
Bunkeya
Kanoni
Kagombo
Luswaka
Likasi
Katofio
Minga
Kiniama
Lubumbashi
Ruashi
Sakania
Elephant
Reserve
Chembe
Mwenda
Tela
Shaba
Mufulira
Chingola
Chililabombwe
Kasumbalesa
Mokambo
Kipushi
Tumbwe
Solwezi

the CAR

16

Inspect your car regularly

Walk around your car and have a good look at it. How do the tyres look? Is the tread still in order? Get someone to help you check that all the lights are working. Open the boot and check whether the spare tyre is properly inflated. Open the bonnet and make sure that everything is in order. Such an inspection may take a little time, but it could save you a lot of inconvenience.

Apply clear nail polish to small scratches on the paintwork of the car to prevent rust.

Overheating

If your car overheats while you are driving, turn the heating in the car up as high as it will go and put the fan on. If you have to stop at a traffic light, put the car in neutral and rev the engine slightly. If the engine is still too hot, it is advisable to pull over somewhere safe and wait for the engine to cool down before opening the bonnet.

Carrying water

Use a hub cap to carry water if nothing else is available. A plastic bag would also be handy.

Separate petrol and water

To separate petrol and water, pour it through chamois leather. Only the petrol will run through.

Keep the fuel filter clean

An engine that is working optimally will ensure the best fuel consumption. Replace the oil regularly and do not wait too long before replacing the air and petrol filters.

When on dirt roads

Keep a plank in the boot in case you need to change a tyre in soft sand.

Dropper for oil

- Use a nose or eye dropper to dispense small amounts of oil in hard-to-reach places.
- Put a drinking straw over the spout of an oil can to make it easier to reach awkward spots.
- Make a paper funnel for pouring oil into the engine.

Keep mats in place

Keep the mats in your car firmly in place by attaching strips of the hooked part of Velcro to the bottom of them. The mats will then stick to the carpeting in the car.

Tar spots

Remove spots of tar on the paintwork with white floor polish, linseed oil or butter.

Tiny scratches

Apply clear nail polish to small scratches on the paintwork of the car to prevent rust.

An engine that's shiny and clean

Use power paraffin to clean the engine as it is not as volatile as petrol. You could also mix ordinary washing powder and water to a paste and apply it to the engine. Leave to stand for a while before rinsing off with hot water.

Clean bumpers

Use shoe polish to clean plastic bumpers.

Shiny dashboard

Keep your car's dashboard looking new by polishing it with petroleum jelly.

Upholstery

Clean leather car seats with a damp cloth, hot water and soft soap. Remove stains from upholstery with a paste of bicarbonate of soda and water. Do not use products that contain ammonia.

Washing warnings

- Do not clean car windows with ammonia because it will remove the UV protective layer from the glass. Rather use a sponge with a small amount of household window soap or a product specially made for car windows with UV protection.
- Dishwashing liquid is not suitable for washing a car because it removes the layer of polish that makes the car shine.

Windscreen wipers

- Apply glycerine to windscreen wiper blades and the rubber around car doors to keep them soft and supple. This also stops the doors freezing closed if your car is parked outside in sub-zero temperatures.
- Place a piece of cardboard between the windscreen and the wipers if the car has to stand outside in exceptionally cold weather.

Fresh-smelling interior

Place a small bag of fabric softener under the driver's seat to keep the car smelling fresh.

Batteries

Apply petroleum jelly to battery heads to prevent corrosion, but be careful not to apply it to the contact surface of the battery terminals. If a battery terminal has already started to corrode, clean it with a small brush.

Wiring

Have the wiring checked out if your car is giving problems, and make sure all the wires in the fuses are in place.

Bumps and scrapes

- Buy special rubber stops for car doors to prevent them being bumped or scratched on opening. Attach sponge pool noodles to the garage wall at door height if the doors keep hitting the wall.
- Hang a tennis ball on a rope from the garage roof that will rest against the windscreen to indicate when the car is in far enough.

When buying second-hand

- Buy a second-hand vehicle from a dealer who abides by the Retail Motor Industry's (RMI) code of conduct or who is a member of the Independent Dealers' Association (IDA).
- Also make sure that the dealer is approved by leading financing companies. Before buying, have the car checked for mechanical soundness by the AA (Automobile Association), and also get them to check whether the vehicle has been reported as stolen.

Finding faults

Get someone who knows about cars to drive your car every now and then. They are often more likely to detect something wrong with the car than you are when you drive it every day. Many problems develop gradually and you may get so used to it that you do not notice the issue any more.

Small dents

Suck small dents out of a car's bodywork using a rubber plunger. Wet the area before pressing the plunger firmly over the dent and pulling it out again with a short, sharp tug.

Raincoat for a distributor

If you want to protect your car's ignition distributor in extremely wet weather, cut off the tips of the fingers of a rubber glove, put the glove over the distributor and pull the spark plug wires through the fingers.

Make an under-car trolley

Use an old ironing board to make your own trolley for working under the car by replacing the legs with castors.

Hole in the exhaust pipe

- Buy exhaust paste from a car-accessories dealer and use it to cover the hole. Cut the top and bottom off a tin that is a bit larger than the exhaust pipe, then cut the tin down the length. Place the tin over the paste with the two sides overlapping. Tie the two pieces together securely using steel clamps made for hosepipes and plastic pipes.
- As a temporary solution, work a piece of green household soap and water between your fingers and use it to patch the hole in the exhaust pipe.

Keep a spare

Always keep a spare fan belt in the car (store it with the spare wheel). In an emergency a piece of stretchy material or a stocking will also work.

Notes

Notes

GREEN hints for the HOME

17

Reduce, reuse, recycle

We have only one earth although we use 1,3. The earth is yours too and your responsibility, and it is important to know the effect of the choices you make.

Save with prepaid electricity

- Using less electricity not only helps reduce CO_2 emissions, it can do wonders for your budget too!
- Install prepaid electricity, which will give you a much better idea of how much electricity you use at which times of day. This will help you control your electricity bill and find solutions to reducing consumption during peak times.

Use the sun

- The sun is hot and free in South Africa, which enjoys one of the highest rates of sunshine per day in the world.
- Consider having solar panels installed for heating.
- Think of ways of using the sun to heat water.
- Use solar panels and/or a solar blanket to heat your swimming pool.
- Hang your washing out to dry in the sun instead of using a tumble dryer.
- Install outdoor lighting that works off solar panels.

Free hot water

- Heat water by filling a 50-litre black bucket or plastic container with water and placing it in a sunny spot. Make sure that there are no chemical deposits in the bucket and buy a new one if you are unsure.
- Roll up a black hose in a single layer in a sunny spot and attach it to the water supply. You should be able to dispense hot water a few times a day.

Good insulation

- Proper insulation will keep a house cool in summer and warm in winter.
- Make sure you find out how the insulation material was manufactured and that it is safe.
- Insulation also helps improve the acoustics of your home.
- Wooden frames in buildings are better insulators than steel ones.

Insulation material

Use old blankets if you do not have other insulation material.

Keep pipes hot

Insulate water pipes by wrapping them in insulation material in such a way that it overlaps slightly.

Scraps of insulation

Place scraps of insulation filling in plastic refuse bags, close the bags and tie them around the water tank or geyser.

Save electricity

Make use of a double adaptor with multiple plug points and its own switch. This will enable you to switch off a number of appliances at once.

Make use of a double adaptor with multiple plug points and its own switch. This will enable you to switch off a number of appliances at once.

Be informed

- When buying a new appliance, find out exactly how much electricity it uses. For example, appliances manufactured in the EU are marked with an A for the lowest consumption and with a D for the highest.
- Make absolutely sure you need an electrical appliance before buying it.
- Buy the right size appliance for your needs: smaller televisions and fridges often use less electricity.

Vacuum-cleaner savings

Clean out the vacuum cleaner bag once a week – this saves electricity. Throw the contents onto your compost heap.

Lighting plan

Choose lights in such a way that you distinguish between general lighting and focus or work lighting. General lighting provides diffuse light through a large area while work lighting provides a focused light. Work lights should be switched on only when needed.

Turn it off!

Switch off the lights when no one is in the room. It is not true that it takes more electricity to switch a light on again than to leave it burning.

Motion detector

Install a motion detector that will switch off the lights automatically after a certain time in places where the lights often get left on unnecessarily, such as in the garage, storeroom or passage.

Reduce water use

Install low-flow aerators on old taps. These are rings of rubber or an artificial material that reduce the flow of water and therefore the amount of water used. They are ideal for shower baths, but serve no purpose if you fill the bath or bucket up to the top, since the tap will stay open until the bath or bucket is full anyway!

Save water

- Use less water by washing the dishes in a basin in the sink.
- Use a twin-tub washing machine. Save the last water from the final rinse and use it for the next load's first wash or for a prewash.
- Use a short cycle or water-saving, economy cycle on the dishwasher.
- Shower into a plastic basin and use the water collected on your garden.

Flush less

Place two bottles of water in a toilet cistern that uses too much water. You could also install a cistern that enables you to control the flush.

Bath and toilet

- Install a water-saving device that lets you use rain water or bath water to flush the toilet.
- Insulate the bath with insulation material such as glass wool (fibreglass) to keep the water hot for longer.
- Install a water-saving showerhead.
- Do not leave taps running unnecessarily.

Get a group of friends together and start a recycling collection point in your area if there is not one at present.

Think about disposal

Every time you buy something, ask yourself how you will dispose of it later. Also try to buy products with less packaging and consider how the packaging will be recycled. Choose paper and glass packaging rather than plastic, if possible.

Recycle your refuse

It is up to you to decide what to do with your waste and how to get rid of it. Find out about recycling depots in your area and which materials and products they accept. Start a compost heap (see page 239 for how to do this) and set up a sorting area. It takes a bit more effort, but you and your environment will benefit in the long term.

What is recyclable?

- Very few materials are not recyclable. However, there are few places that recycle problem materials such as polymers. Contact recycling organisations in your area and find out what is realistic and achievable to recycle.
- There are many websites with information on recycling. Examples are:
  - The National Recycling Forum: http://www.recycling.co.za
  - My Green Choices: http://www.mygreenchoices.co.za
  - Urbansprout: http://www.urbansprout.co.za
  - The Plastics Federation of South Africa: http://www.plasticsinfo.co.za
  - Collect a Can: http://www.collectacan.co.za
  - Paperpickup: http://www.paperpickup.co.za
  - Glass Recycling Company: http://www.theglassrecyclingcompany.co.za
  - Going Green: http://www.goinggreen.co.za

Green challenge

- Get a group of friends and neighbours together and start a recycling collection point in your area if there is not one at present.

- Make your children and others in your household aware of how important recycling is, and vote with your wallet: buy items in recyclable packaging.
- Take your own shopping bags with you when you go grocery shopping.

Second-hand clothes

Read the washing instructions when buying second-hand clothes. An item of clothing that has to be dry-cleaned could end up costing you more than a new one in the long term.

Buying second-hand books

Second-hand books are a good recycling initiative, but you should check the quality:

- Sniff the book for mould – it is difficult to get rid of.
- Page through the book to check that all the pages are there and intact.
- Check that the spine of the book is intact.
- Look out for water damage.

Book exchange

Set up a magazine and book club in which members can swap and share their reading matter.

Second-hand is not always best

Think very carefully about buying the following items second hand:

- Children's car seats: the safety requirements for such seats change continually and, what is more, the seat could have been damaged internally in an accident.
- Old painted toys: the paint could contain lead.
- Electrical appliances with suspect wiring: they could cause a short circuit.
- Old fridges and washing machines: most of them use twice as much electricity as new, modern products.
- Hairdryers without built-in protection against electrocution.

Line shelves

If you are loathe to buy expensive paper or contact plastic, use newspaper or old wrapping paper to line the bottoms of recycling containers, drawers and shelves. In the old days, grandma would cut pretty patterns in the paper before putting it on the shelves.

Doing the washing

- Wash clothes at a lower temperature in order to save electricity and water. If the clothes are very soiled, soak them beforehand in water and green household soap.
- Only wash full loads in the washing machine. A full load uses the same amount of electricity as half a load, and proportionally more water.

Two for one

Place a steel plate that is at least 5 mm thick over two of the burners on your gas stove. Then light only one of them. The burner will heat the entire plate and you will be able to place a second pot on it without having to light another burner.

Newspaper for coal

Soak newspaper in water, squeeze it into balls until all the moisture has been removed and then leave to dry out. Use the balls in a coal stove if the coal or wood runs out.

Three questions to ask when buying food:

- How was the product made?
- How did the product reach me?
- How much does the product cost the environment?

Takeaways

Take your own food container when ordering takeaways and ask the restaurant to pack your meal in it. There is less waste and you can be sure the food will not leak or spill during your journey home.

Notes

BIBLIOGRAPHY

Bakker, Y. 2010. *Wonen is een werkwoord: handboek voor eigenwijs wonen.* Page 144. Utrecht: Kosmos Uitgevers.

Barclay, L.; Grosvenor, M.; Soerjadi, I. et al. 2008. *Groen leven voor dummies.* Page 297. Amsterdam: Pearson Addison Weasley.

Bergs, J.A. 2004. *Gezond wonen: gids voor gezond leven in huis.* Page 80. Zutphen: Roodbont.

Berry, S.; Van Benthum, A.; Boonstra, S. et al. 2008. *Groen leven in eigen huis en tuin.* Page 127. Baarn: Forte Uitgevers.

Binsch, P. & Van der Graaff, A. 1997. *Zo doe je dat! Meer dan 10 000 tips voor huis, tuin, hobby en vrije tijd.* Page 527. Amsterdam & Brussels: The Reader's Digest.

Buns, S. & Stammer, J. 1996. *101 Tuintips wat mijn grootvader nog wist.* Page 71. Aartselaar: Zuidnederlandse Uitgeverij N.V.

Hartemink, D. 2010. *Dekselse dames.* Page 98. Hilversum: F.C. Klap.

Haynes, A. 2004. *De complete huishoudbijbel.* Page 287. Aartselaar: Zuidnederlandse Uitgeverij N.V.

Hessayon, D.G. 1994. *Het complete tuinboek.* Page 128. Haarlem: Schuyt & Co Uitgevers en Importeurs BV.

Jantra, H. 1988. *Compleet handboek kamer planten.* Page 303. Aartselaar: Zuidnederlandse Uitgeverij N.V.

Kay, S. 2006. *No more clutter.* Page 224. London: Hodder Mobius.

Kos en Kookkuns. 1984. Page 280. Pretoria: Government Printer.

Kritzinger, L. 1993. *Huisgenoot wenke wat werk.* Page 191. Cape Town: Human & Rousseau.

Middeldorp, M. 2005. *Hoe schoon is jouw huis? Tips voor supersopgenot.* Page 176. Baarn: Tririon.

Monkau, S. & Göbel, I. 2009. *Ecowinst voor woningen: handboek voor een goed energielabel.* Page 111. Arnhem: Ecotrigger.

Phillips, B. 1989. *'n Praktiese gids vir Suid-Afrika. Wenke vir die huis.* Page 304. Cape Town: Tafelberg.

Psilakis, N. & M. 1998. *Olive oil: The secret of good health with advice on its correct use.* Page 175. Crete: Typokreta.

Tourmente, N. 2008. *Groenten en kruiden kweken in potten en bakken.* Page 119. Aartselaar: Oosterhout.

Van der Meij, M. 2006. *Oma weet raad.* Page 191, Soest: Verba.

Visser, T. 1995. *Dit werk!* Page 173. Cape Town: Tafelberg.

http://www.praxis.nl/klussen

http://www.marthastewart.com/

INDEX